THE *Stanze* OF ANGELO POLIZIANO

Translated by DAVID QUINT

The Pennsylvania State University Press
University Park, Pennsylvania

For Louise Clubb, Robert Durling, and John Freccero

The Italian text of the *Stanze* presented here is
the critical edition of Vincenzo Pernicone (Turin:
Loescher Editore, 1954), reprinted with the gracious
permission of the publisher.

First published in 1979 by The University of Massachusetts Press

First paperback edition published in 1993 by The Pennsylvania State
University Press, Barbara Building, Suite C, University Park, PA 16802

Library of Congress Cataloging-in-Publication Data

    Poliziano, Angelo, 1454–1494.
    [Poems. Selections. English]
    The Stanze of Angelo Poliziano / translated by David Quint.
        p.   cm.
    Includes bibliographical references.
    ISBN 0-271-00937-3
    1. Poliziano, Angelo, 1454–1494—Translations into English
I. Title.
PQ4630.P5A2613 1993
851 ' . 2—dc20   92-35532
                                             CIP

Contents

Preface

This translation attempts to make accessible to English-speaking readers a major document of Renaissance culture. My aim has been a clear and literal rendering of the *Stanze*. I have chosen to translate Poliziano's octave stanza into prose paragraphs instead of verse. Given the technical demands of the stanza form, a translation into English octaves is likely to remain close to the spirit rather than to the letter of the Italian verse. The translation does not pretend to be a substitute, but rather a supplement to the original, which is printed across the page.

The Italian text of the *Stanze* presented here is the critical edition of Vincenzo Pernicone (Turin: Loescher Editore, 1954), reprinted with the gracious permission of the publisher. I have on two occasions preferred the alternate readings of Natalino Sapegno (Rome: Ateneo, 1967). (1) The opening verse of Book I, stanza 77 reads: *Cotal milizia e tuoi figli accompagna* (Pernicone: *Con tal milizia e suoi figli accompagna*. (2) In Book II, stanza 20, I have followed Sapegno in capitalizing *Viltà* and *Libertate* in verses 1 and 3.

This translation project was first undertaken in a Yale College course taught by John Freccero. Further work and research were sponsored by a Robert C. Bates Travelling Fellowship. I have received valuable advice and criticism on the text of the translation from Thomas Bergin and Louise Clubb. The introduction has benefited from the comments of many generous friends and readers: Louise Clubb, A. Bartlett Giamatti, Tony Grafton, Thomas Greene, Arthur Kinney, James Nohrnberg, and Thomas Roche. My father, Howard Quint, gave me constant encouragement and experienced editorial advice.

I owe a special debt of gratitude to Robert Durling, who is the true *miglior fabbro* of this book. His emendations and advice have amounted to a virtual course in the art of translation, and his meticulous work has removed many mistakes and added polish to the manuscript. What errors or inelegancies may remain are my own.

Introduction

Angelo Poliziano (1454–1494), the most brilliant humanist of Renaissance
Florence, was born Angelo Ambrogini in the Tuscan community of Montepulciano. From his native town, *Mons Politianus*, he derived the Latinate
surname that was the trademark of a Renaissance humanist—he is known in
English as Politian. His childhood was traumatized by violence and privation. In
1464, his father was killed in a local feud of vengeance. The ten-year-old Angelo
came to Florence where, living in loneliness and poverty, he immersed himself in
the study of Latin. In 1469, he began courses in Greek at the Studio, the
Florentine university, and the following year saw the appearance of his translation
of Book II of the *Iliad* into Latin hexameters—no small accomplishment for the
precocious scholar of sixteen. Both this work and his subsequent translation of
Book III were dedicated to Lorenzo de' Medici, the young head of the great
banking family and the de facto ruler of Florence. By 1473, the young poet had
entered the service of the Medici household as Lorenzo's protégé and intimate
companion. Two years later he became the tutor of Lorenzo's sons. But Clarice
Orsini, Lorenzo's wife, preferred a religious rather than a classical education for
their children. Long-standing differences between mother and teacher resulted
in Poliziano's dismissal in 1479. Later in the same year, he fell out of favor
with Lorenzo himself. Following a six-month, self-imposed exile from Florence,
he re-entered Lorenzo's good graces and accepted the post of lecturer at the
Studio, where he produced a series of superb commentaries and translations
of the classics. His scholarly activity culminated in the 1489 publication of his
Miscellanea, a collection of one hundred expanded textual notes, a masterpiece
of erudition and of a meticulous philological method which laid down many of
the essential principles of modern editorial practice. He acquired an international
reputation as the outstanding classical scholar of his age, and his Latin poetry
continued to be prized and read beside that of the ancient authors well into the
age of Alexander Pope. Poliziano had taken minor orders, and his letters to
Lorenzo and Lorenzo's son and successor, Piero, contain frequent petitions for

available ecclesiastical benefices. He devoted himself to the occupations of scholarship, poetry and the acquisition of wealth until his death in 1494, two years after the death of Lorenzo. In his last days, Poliziano was caught up by the spiritual revival of Savonarola. He was buried as a penitent in the cowl of a Dominican friar.

Poliziano's own achievement as a man of letters and the patronage of the Medici elevated him to a central position in the intellectual and artistic circles of Laurentine Florence. He was a cultural celebrity who knew everybody and whom everybody wanted to know. One of his earliest friends and benefactors was the philosopher Marsilio Ficino, who wrote to Lorenzo in praise of the ' "homericum adolescentem" then translating the *Iliad*. Ficino himself was engaged in his life-long project of translating the newly available works of Plato, as well as the writings of Plotinus, "Hermes Trismegistus," and other Neoplatonic thinkers. Ficino evolved his own syncretic Platonic philosophy which stressed the life of contemplation and the intellective union of the soul with God. His famous commentary on Plato's *Symposium*, the *De Amore*, outlined a theory of Platonic love in which human love is the first step in the contemplative ascent toward the enjoyment of divine Beauty. Although Poliziano did not share such Platonic enthusiasms—his own modest philosophical interests were directed toward problems in Aristotelian terminology—he maintained a cordial relationship with Ficino and, after 1479, became a close friend for life of the other great figure of Florentine Neoplatonism, the young Count Giovanni Pico della Mirandola.[1] Both Ficino's philosophy and Poliziano's poetry influenced the work of the painter Sandro Botticelli. The *Stanze* are celebrated as the literary source for several of Botticelli's most famous pictures. *The Birth of Venus* in the Uffizi Gallery in Florence probably drew inspiration from the description in Book I, 99–101. *Venus and Mars* in London's National Gallery may derive from octave 122, while a phrase in octave 68,

where lascivious Zephyr flies behind Flora and decks the green grass with flowers . . .

suggests the iconography of the Uffizi *Primavera*. According to Vasari and Condivi, Poliziano gave advice on classical subjects to the adolescent Michelangelo, whom Lorenzo was the first to "discover" and patronize.[2] Lorenzo was himself a poet of considerable talent. In his *Commento*, a series of sonnets and prose commentaries, he defended the literary use of the Italian vernacular instead of Latin, and in the 1470s he presided over a revival of Italian verse. Lorenzo sponsored the comic poet Luigi Pulci and his rambling, often brilliant burlesque epic, the *Morgante Maggiore*, a work to which Poliziano appears to have lent a guiding hand: Pulci ends the *Morgante* with a flattering eulogy of his good "Angel" from Montepulciano.[3]

Lorenzo probably encouraged and certainly influenced Poliziano's own efforts in Italian poetry. The *ballate*, the best of Poliziano's lyrics, share the spontaneity and charm of Lorenzo's dance and carnival poems. Poliziano immediately mastered the difficulties of Italian versification, and gave to the octave—the conventional stanza of narrative verse—a new suppleness and capacity for expression that would be exploited in the following centuries by Ariosto, Tasso, and Marino, the "great tradition" of Italian epic poetry. Despite this technical facility, Poliziano's vernacular works are relatively few in number when compared to his large poetic output in Latin. Most of his Italian poetry is light and occasional; he claims to have dashed off the *Orfeo*, the first secular Italian drama, in the space of two days during his 1480 visit to Mantua. Good humanist that he was, Poliziano preferred to write his serious verse in Latin and—more in the way of an exercise in Greek. The high style and erudition of the *Stanze* are a unique event in Poliziano's career as an Italian poet. When he left off work on the *Stanze* in 1478, he was twenty-four years old.

The *Stanze Cominciate per la Giostra del Magnifico Giuliano de' Medici* celebrate the Florentine tournament of 1475, won by Lorenzo's younger brother, Giuliano. The Medici sponsored the event and Giuliano's victory must have surprised no one: Lorenzo had won a similar joust in 1469. Both festivals, occasioned by treaties of peace with Venice, were symbolic expressions of civic order in a Florence subject to Medici hegemony. The nature of the tournament—martial combat brought under ceremonial constraint—underscored the political significance of the events.

In 1469 Lorenzo, the banker's son turned aristocrat, rode into the lists in a fabulously costly garment encrusted with jewels and pearls. He wore a scarf embroidered with fresh and withered roses. On his standard, the painter Verrocchio depicted branches of laurel. By the lucky coincidence of his name, Lorenzo (Laurentius-Laurus-Lauro) had appropriated the eternal evergreen from Petrarch's Laura and made it his personal emblem. The standard bore the French words, *Le Tems Revient*, echoing verses 4 through 7 of Vergil's *Fourth Eclogue*, which prophesy the return to earth of a Golden Age of peace. The symbolism does not seem difficult: in a world of mutability (the roses), Lorenzo and the Medici are a constant; they promise peace and renewal to Florence and her citizens.[4] In the tournament Lorenzo, ever the astute diplomat and propagandist, rode three different horses, tokens of friendship from the King of Naples and the dukes of Milan and Ferrara. An account of the 1469 joust appears in a minor work of Luigi Pulci, *La Giostra*, which set the poetic precedent for the *Stanze*.

The 1475 tournament was attended by Simonetta Cattaneo, the lovely young wife of Marco Vespucci, cousin of the famous explorer Amerigo. Simonetta captivated Florence with her beauty, and her death one year later produced universal mourning and a flood of elegies from the poets of the city. The nature of her relationship with Giuliano is the subject of conjecture. That the young Medici's passion was real is witnessed by a letter from Piero Vespucci, Simonetta's father-in-law, who writes of having sent the distraught Giuliano some dresses belonging to the dead woman.[5] Lorenzo, too, seems to have fallen in love with Simonetta, and he begins his *Commento* with an account of her death.[6]

In our city, there died a lady who generally moved all the Florentine people to pity; it is no great marvel, for she was truly adorned with as much beauty and gentle kindness as any lady before her. And among her other outstanding gifts she had such a sweet and attractive manner, that all the men who had any familiar acquaintance with her believed that she loved them deeply. Moreover, the ladies and the young women of her own age not only did not envy this most excellent among her other virtues, but highly extolled and praised her beauty and kindness, so that it seemed impossible to believe that so many men loved her without jealousy, and that so many women praised her without envy.

Poliziano for his part had begun to celebrate Simonetta while she was still alive, making her the heroine of the *Stanze*. Her untimely death in 1476 necessitated her resurrection as Fortune in Book II.

But a greater calamity overtook the Medici and their court poet. Despite the rhetoric of the tournament, civic order in Florence was precarious. In 1478 a conspiracy headed by members of the Pazzi family sought to assassinate Lorenzo and Giuliano while the brothers attended Mass. Giuliano fell under the murderers' knives. Though wounded, Lorenzo escaped and the conspiracy failed to wrest the city from Medici control. The death of the hero proved too much for Poliziano's poem. The *Stanze* were left unfinished.

After invocations to Love, and to Lorenzo the Laurel (Book I, stanzas 1-7), the action of the poem opens in a pseudo-classical landscape around Florence. Here Giuliano, his name Latinized to Julio (Julius), lives as a hunter, close to nature. An adolescent, he is ignorant of love, and an angry Cupid decides to punish him for his mockery of lovers (8-24). As Julio enters a forest to hunt, the god places a white doe in his path (25-32). Giving chase to the animal, Julio comes to a clearing where the deer vanishes and a beautiful "nymph" appears in its place (33-37). She reveals her name, Simonetta; she is married and lives in Florence (38-54). She leaves and Julio returns home a changed man, desperately in love (55-57). The rest of Book I is taken up with a description of the garden and palace of Venus on Cyprus; its primary literary source is Claudian's *Epithalamium* (Appendix 1). Poliziano has added the description of the doors sculpted by Vulcan with their mythological scenes of love (97-119). Cupid, meantime, flies back to the garden where he finds his mother on her couch with Mars (120-25).

In Book II, Cupid discusses with Venus the amorous fate of Laurel and Julio. He will take pity on Laurel, who has been faithful to the rule of love. But Julio will have to prove himself in battle in order to gain the hand of Simonetta (II, 1-15). Venus sends out the little cupids to wound all the noble young men of Florence and make them eager to bear arms for love (16-21). Meanwhile she dispatches Pasithea to obtain a dream from the god of sleep (22-26). The dream is intended for Julio: in a vision that owes much to Petrarch's *Triumph of Chastity*, he sees Simonetta overpower Cupid and tie him to Minerva's olive tree, apparently symbolizing a victory of chastity and reason over love. The goddess Glory then descends and disarms Simonetta. Glory and Julio fly off to the field of battle, where Julio carries the day. But on his return he finds Simonetta enveloped in a dark cloud. She emerges as Fortune and as his personal Genius to govern his life and eternalize them both (27–37). On awakening, Julio prays to Minerva, Glory, and Cupid for victory, both in battle and in love (38–46). Here the poem abruptly stops, never reaching the action of the tournament itself.

The transfer of contemporary events into a classical setting and the celebration of the patron as a mythological hero were common strategies of Renaissance court poets. Poliziano sustains his fiction with constant literary allusion. As the learned commentaries of Carducci and Sapegno attest, there is scarcely a verse in the *Stanze* that does not imitate an earlier text, either from classical or Italian literature. The description of Simonetta is a good example of Poliziano's procedure:

From her eyes there flashes a honeyed calm in which Cupid hides his torch; wherever she turns those amorous eyes, the air about her becomes serene. Her face, sweetly painted with privet and roses, is filled with heavenly joy; every breeze is hushed before her divine speech, and every little bird sings out in its own language. [I, 44]

Simonetta's sweet flashing eyes recall at least four classical passages (Horace C. II, 12, 15; Propertius IV, 8, 55; Ovid *Ars Amatoria* II, 721; Claudian *Epithalamium*, 41), as well as the opening lines of sonnet 258 of Petrarch's *Canzoniere*. Her calming effect on the air imitates Petrarch's sonnet 192. The happiness which fills her face echoes Dante's description of Beatrice in *Paradiso* XXIII, 23. Her complexion of privet and roses derives from Claudian's *De Raptu Proserpinae* II, 130. The charming final line about the singing birds is almost directly quoted from a lyric of Guido Cavalcanti. Simonetta, like the octave itself, has become an assemblage of poetic allusions. Her historical identity is subsumed into a fictional character composed out of a series of pre-existent literary types.

This "bookish" method of composition may account for the condescension with which the *Stanze* (and the humanist poetry of the Italian Renaissance of which they are typical) have been treated by the central tradition of modern Italian literary criticism. The critics of the post-Risorgimento, who never forgave the humanists their Latinity—a betrayal of the national popular idiom—nevertheless admired the plastic beauty of verse and images imitated from classical models. The allusive texture of humanist literature was understood to have a primarily formal rather than thematic rationale; indeed the humanists' thought and subject matter seemed relatively unimportant. Francesco De Sanctis (1817–1883), the dean of nineteenth-century Italian critics, wrote:

Poliziano had an exquisite feeling for form with complete indifference to content. The temple was empty: Apollo entered it and filled it with images and harmonies.[7]

De Sanctis's formulations were easily assimilated into the aesthetic theory of Benedetto Croce (1866–1952) who banished "content," in the sense of intellectual concepts and historical ideas, from all artistic experience.[8] Contemporary Italian criticism is still grappling with Croce's formalist legacy.

Such criticism fails to consider the humanists' stated intentions. In his celebrated letter to Paolo Cortese, Poliziano inveighs against a superficial classicism, comparing to apes and parrots those authors who scatter classical phrases throughout their writing solely to give the appearance of learning. Furthermore, he insists that each writer develop his own personal style, refusing to be strait-jacketed by strict adherence to the diction and style of the Golden Age Latin of Cicero and Vergil:

Some one says to me, "You don't express yourself as if you were Cicero." What of that? I am not Cicero. I express myself.[9]

This statement should not be misinterpreted: it is in fact a conservative defense against Cortese's Ciceronianism, and upholds the wide-ranging classical imitation that had been the staple method of learning employed in the earlier humanists' educational program. From his reading the Renaissance schoolboy compiled a personal *florilegium*, or notebook anthology, of catchy phrases, aphorisms, metaphors, and rhetorical figures from which he was to form his own speech and writing. The common image used to describe such stylistic creation was that of the bee which mixes into honey the nectar gathered from many and various flowers. The true *doctus*, the learned man, exploiting a deep and wide erudition, could find the apposite classical allusion or model for any occasion. For Poliziano, literary imitation did not limit, but rather expanded the range of individual expression.

By imitation, moreover, the humanist took his own place in literary history. The historicist criticism of Poliziano's *Miscellanea*—which comments upon a given classical text by citing its sources, models, and parallel passages in ancient literature—is built into his poetic method.[10] When Poliziano draws a poetic figure such as the detail of Simonetta's flashing eyes not from one but from a combination of literary sources, he recapitulates the history of the figure. Propertius imitated Horace; Ovid imitated Propertius and Horace; Claudian imitated Ovid, Propertius, and Horace; Petrarch imitated the classical poets in Italian; finally Poliziano imitates both them and Petrarch. The meanings of the *Stanze* depend upon a continuous literary tradition which their poetic text reveals to be the product of a history of imitation. The literary historian who traces the imitated figure to its original context understands poetry as a human artifact whose meaning depends upon the historical circumstances of its author. Yet the very continuity achieved by the imitation and repetition of poetic meaning over the centuries may lend that meaning an aura of timelessness and autonomy from human history. In the *Nutricia*, the longest of his Latin poems, Poliziano borrows an image from Plato's *Ion* to describe an alternative, "sacralized" version of literary history: in an unbroken line, each poet is inspired by his predecessors, joined like a chain of magnetized iron filings derived from the original loadstone, Homer, whose inspiration was divine.[11] The divine inspiration of the *Nutricia* may operate as a metaphor for the human imitation studied by the *Miscellanea*, but it reinvests poetic meaning with an ahistorical authority that the *Miscellanea* excludes. Poliziano probably did not believe in the *Nutricia*'s myth of inspiration; but one side of his personality may have wanted to believe in it, hoping to find in poetry a stability of meaning made impossible by the flux and contingency of history.[12] To join in the chain of inspiration of the *Nutricia* would mean to suppress the literary individuality upheld by Poliziano in his letter to Cortese: the inspired poet is merely the vessel in which a timeless meaning is conveyed. On the other hand, the imitative poet who achieves individuality by acknowledging his own historical place in a literary tradition must also acknowledge the temporal instability of his discourse. The conflict between poetry and history in Poliziano's thought is not resolved; rather it is manifested in the thematic enterprise of the *Stanze*, which is the transformation of historical events into poetic myth.

From the outset of the poem, love displaces the tournament as the center of interest.

you ennoble whatever you regard, for no baseness can exist within your breast; Love, whose subject I am forever, now lend your hand to my low intellect. [I, 2]

The nature of love is a problem as difficult for the characters as for the reader of the *Stanze*. Although Poliziano has frequent recourse to the motifs and erotic psychology of Ficino's *De Amore*, only Julio's tripartite prayer to Minerva, Glory, and Love at the end of Book II bears the suggestion of a Neoplatonic contemplative ascent.[13] The human love of the *Stanze* is decidedly earthbound and derives from an earlier tradition of Italian literature. The passage cited above recalls the thirteenth-century poetry of Guido Guinizelli and the early Dante of the *Vita Nuova*: according to the doctrine of the *dolce stil novo*, love transforms and ennobles the lover.[14] In a variation of this theme, Boccaccio, in a tale of the *Decameron*, recounts the story of a Cyprian youth, Cimone, whose ignorance and coarseness are his father's despair until the young man falls in love; then,

because of the love which he bore Efigenia, not only did he change his harsh and rustic voice into a citizenly and mannerly one, but he became master of dance and song, and he became expert and bold in riding and martial skills, those of the sea as well as those of the land. And in short, so that I do not go on reciting each particular of his virtue, he had not completed one quarter of a year before he became better graced and better mannered, with more individual virtues, than any other youth on the island of Cyprus. [V, 1]

A similar erotic scenario is acted out in the *Stanze*. The poem celebrates love less as a movement toward contemplative experience than as the educative link between the individual and the culture of his society. Love is the catalyst which transforms human potential into *humanitas*.

The *Stanze* document Julio's progress from adolescence to adulthood. Julio's pastoral enthusiasm, his rejection of love and sexuality are an attempt to postpone the life-crisis: he is the child who refuses to grow up. He finds an analogy to his own semiprimitive existence in the mythical Golden Age that preceded civilization:

'The evil thirst for cruel gold had not yet entered the beautiful world; the happy people lived in liberty, the fields, though unplowed, were plentiful. Fortune, envious of their peace, broke all laws and cast pity aside; lust entered human hearts and that madness which the people, in their misery, call love.' [I, 21]

The advent of love forces upon the adolescent an acknowledgment of his place in a generational sequence just as the loss of an Edenic Golden Age signaled the beginning of history. But man is a historical being, and Julio's pastoral is merely the evasion of his temporal destiny. The classical texture of the poem suggests a more serious regression. The description of Julio:

How many nymphs sighed for him! But the amorous nymphs could never make the arrogant boy yield, nor could his cold breast be warmed. [I, 10]

echoes Ovid's *Metamorphoses*:

multi illum iuvenes, multae cupiere puellae;
sed fuit in tenera tam dura superbia forma,
nulli illum iuvenes, nullae tetigere puellae.

many youths, many girls desired him; but in his delicate figure dwelt such harsh pride that no youths, no girls ever moved him. [III, 353–55]

And the cry of the indignant lover whom Julio has scorned:

But one poor wretch whose sinews were being consumed by ardent flames cried out to heaven: 'Let just disdain move you, Love, let him at least believe by experience!' [I, 22]

has its model in the same Ovidian passage:

inde manus aliquis despectus ad aethera tollens
'sic amet ipse licet, sic non potiatur amato!'

then one of the scorned lovers, lifting his hands toward heaven, prayed, 'So let him love and not obtain the one he loves!' [III, 404–5]

The subject of Ovid's discourse is Narcissus: Julio's pastoral is not only timeless but self-absorbing. The alternative to the erotic bond is not the freedom that

Julio envisions but ultimately an egocentric prison. His retreat from Florence, from adult relationships and responsibilities, is opposed to the human community founded on altruistic love. Love will lead Julio back to the city, to the tournament quite literally in the midst of the civic arena.

Moreover, Julio's hunt belies any benign pastoral relationship between man and nature. The people of the vegetarian Golden Age lived on acorns and the spontaneous produce of unplowed fields. In the historical world man struggles and kills to subsist. The hunt, which begins as a picturesque description of an aristocratic pastime, becomes increasingly anarchic in character:

with such horror, Megaera, gluttonous for Latin blood, sounded the Tartarean trumpet. [I, 28]

In such a way, the ferocious Centaur goes to hunt through the snowy forests of Pelion or Haemus, chasing every beast from its den: now he kills the bear, now menaces the lion; the braver the beast the further within the woods it hides, blood turns to ice inside each heart; the woods tremble, and every plant gives way, he beats down or uproots the trees, or shatters their branches. [I, 32]

The source of both of these passages is Book VII of the *Aeneid*. Megaera's sister fury, Alecto, incites the Rutulians to battle against Aeneas (511–15) while the Centaur simile describes two military leaders in the Rutulian catalogue of arms (674–77). The noise and confusion of the hunt are set allusively against the outbreak of civil war in Vergil's Italy. The hunt culminates with the image of Julio-as-Centaur, running rampant and cutting a swath of destruction through the forest.[15] The relationship of the self-centered adolescent to the exterior world expresses itself in violence and brute force.

To portray the process of Julio's socialization, Poliziano employs the great classical poetic form of transformation, the Ovidian metamorphosis. But the traditional terms of the metamorphosis—man changed into beast or plant—are here reversed. Cupid's white doe disappears and Simonetta takes its place. The destructive energy of the hunt is harnessed and channeled by the impulse of love. The confused entanglement of the woods gives way to the meadow calmed by Simonetta's presence, prefiguring the garden of Venus in the second half of Book I. The simile used to describe the change wrought in Julio is the bestiary anecdote of the tiger, here derived from Claudian (*De Raptu Proserpinae* III, 263–68).

Even so an enraged tigress, from whose rocky den a hunter has stolen her cherished young, follows him through the Hyrcanian woods, thinking soon to bloody her claws; then pauses before the vain reflection of a mirroring water, before the reflection that resembles her children; and while the fool is enamored of that sight, the hunter flies away. [I, 39]

The roles of hunter and hunted have been reversed. In Claudian, the simile describes Ceres searching for her abducted daughter Proserpina; here the stolen cubs may intimate the loss of Julio's childhood. But the startling detail of the mirror demonstrates the particular aptness of Poliziano's choice of classical models. The earlier suggestions of Narcissism are transmuted as Simonetta becomes the mirror in which Julio finds his self-image. The following passage by Marsilio Ficino on the psychology of love may serve as a gloss:

Moreover, a lover imprints a likeness of the loved one upon his soul, and so the soul of the lover becomes a mirror in which is reflected the image of the loved one. Thereupon, when the loved one recognizes himself in the lover, he is forced to love him.[16]

The movement out of egocentrism to self-consciousness—a recognition of self in the other—spells the end of Julio's independence. At the end of their conversation—during which Simonetta reveals herself as a nymph of domesticity, a respectable married churchgoer—the hero has relinquished both individuality and freedom:

Already he feels himself one among the other lovers [I, 57]

before you were your own man, now you belong to Love, now you are bound, before you were unfettered. [I, 59]

Again Ficino's treatise on love seems relevant to the poem's concerns.

To this is added the fact that neither human nor animal love can ever exist without an accompanying indignation. Who is not outraged by him who has taken his soul from him? For as liberty is the most pleasing of all conditions, so servitude is the most unbearable. And so you love and hate the beautiful at the same time.[17]

The subordination of the self is implicit both in love and in the individual's relationship to the human community. Julio's dread of erotic subjection is not seen as necessarily mistaken but rather as immature; the surrender of self-sufficiency is the key step toward adulthood. The episode closes with the relief of Julio's companions at his safe return to his Florentine home:

But soon each raised his brow in gladness, seeing safe so dear a charge: so Ceres appeared, after she had found her sweet daughter below in the realm of Death. [I, 67]

Julio is restored to his anxious family but, like the ravished Proserpina whom Ceres sought, the former Julio no longer exists. Leaving behind his pastoral for the historical world of the city, the hero has crossed from innocence to experience.

The *Stanze* now move with Cupid to the garden of Venus on Cyprus. The garden, produced by the marriage of Venus to Vulcan, the divine artificer and founder of cities, suggests again the nexus between love and civilization.[18] In its timeless, controlled laboratory atmosphere, the domesticating influence of love is examined first in the animal world, then among the gods themselves.

In contrast to the violence of Julio's hunt, peace reigns among the beasts of the garden. Cupid stated earlier, "I cause the tiger to lose its rage, the dragon its hiss, the lion its savage roar" (I, 24). Here the law of the jungle is annulled:

Beside the Libyan lion, the stag raises its hooves to embrace his mate; in the meadow where spring smiles most, one rabbit nestles with another; safe from hounds, the simple hares go in groups on their amorous chase; so does Love, when he desires, abate ancient hatred and natural fear inside their breasts. [I, 88]

But another kind of animal strife remains—the mating combat:

The timid deer do battle and become bold for their beloved paramour; with striped hides, the fierce, raging tigers furiously rush to wound each other; proud, roaring lions lash their tails and fight face to face with fiery eyes. [I, 87]

The struggle between contending males provides an analogue to the forthcoming tournament. As the beasts turn from warfare to amorous jousts, Simonetta inspires Julio to abandon the hunt and ride into the lists along with other young Florentines whom Venus's cupids will incite to take part in the games of Mars (II, 16–21). In the background lies the cessation of hostilities with Venice: Julio's course is reproduced in the larger political world.

Pacification and erotic subordination merge at the divine level in the union of Venus and Mars, the culminating tableau of Book I. Poliziano's source is the opening of the *De Rerum Natura* (see appendix 3a). Praying for the end of the Roman civil wars, Lucretius made the domination of Mars by Venus an image of universal harmony and *concordia discors*, a meaning which carried over into Ficino's astrological interpretation of the myth (see appendix 3b).[19] Ficino compares Mars and Cupid in another passage.

It is in this way that the power of Cupid differs from the force of Mars; indeed it is in this way that military power and love differ: the general possesses others through himself; the lover takes possession of himself through another. . . . [20]

Ficino's mythography neatly expresses the poem's dichotomy between self-centered irascibility and altruistic love. Cupid explicitly compares Julio the hunter to the Mars who loses his belligerence when recumbent in the lap of Venus (II, 11). Simonetta is to Julio as Venus is to Mars. Human history finds its parallel in the mythic, universal order.

But the mythological scenes sculpted on the doors of the temple of Venus depict a converse movement, a descent from the divine to the human. Vulcan's panels divide into three groups: the birth of love among the gods (I, 97–103); love between the gods and men (105–12); and human love (114–19).

Vulcan's Panels (I, 99–119)

Divinity (the goddess)	Venus is born (99–102)	Venus ascends (103)
Divinity-Humanity (gods and men)	Jupiter, Neptune Saturn and Apollo descend to earth (105–9)	Ganymede and Ariadne are deified (107, 110–12)
Humanity	Hercules unmanned (114)	Polyphemus humanized (115–18)

Each of these three groups of panels contains a double movement: descent followed by ascent. Edgar Wind has argued that the extended description of the birth of Venus from the dismembered Uranus should be read in terms of contemporary Neoplatonic thought as the dispersal of the divine One into the mortal world of history and multiplicity. "But the descent and diffusion of the divine power are followed by its resurrection, when the Many are 'recollected' into the One."[21] Poliziano depicts such a resurrection—the restoration of the unity of the One—in the apotheosis of Venus in stanza 103. The divine must enter the world in the form of Beauty so that men may, in turn, ascend to the divine source of beauty through contemplation. In the second series of panels, the gods are metamorphosed down the scale of being into beasts, while their human loves move upward to become as gods. Wind identifies the deified Ganymede and Ariadne as traditional figures of Neoplatonic contemplative rapture.[22]

The final panels (114–18) use the descent-ascent pattern to depict the effects of an exclusively human love in the erotic abasement of Hercules and the erotic domestication of Polyphemus. Hercules may embody the highest heroic achievement, while the monstrous Polyphemus appears subhuman: the love which degrades Hercules and yet "uplifts" Polyphemus operates on a median level between the noble and bestial sides of human nature. This de-Platonized love, which retains only the up and down trajectories and none of the contemplative ideology of the earlier panels, corresponds to the human love which is the subject matter of the *Stanze*. Hercules and Polyphemus restate the central debate of the poem: does love debilitate or ennoble? The example of the transvestite Hercules in the service of Omphale would confirm Julio's worst fears of subjugation, and presents an ironic version of the conjunction of Mars and Venus. Imitated from *Metamorphoses* XIII, the savage Polyphemus who is turned into a lovesick, bumpkin suitor of Galatea seems to be a comic parallel to the wild hunter Julio domesticated by his love for Simonetta. But, according to Ovid's story, Polyphemus's erotic conversion is of short duration; spurned by Galatea, the jealous Cyclops kills her lover Acis. Vulcan-Poliziano lightly hints at the ensuing catastrophe by ending the representation with Galatea's derision of her primitive serenader. The final panels on Vulcan's doors raise all over again those disturbing questions about human love which the larger poem seems to have answered.

The discontinuity between the Platonic pattern and the human reality of love which emerges in the downward reading of Vulcan's panels suggests the difficulty of applying any mythic prototype to human history, a difficulty which, in turn, raises doubts about the *Stanze*'s entire literary undertaking. The poem begins with the experience of the human characters, Julio and Simonetta, and then proceeds to seek a mythic analogue in the higher, divine realm of the garden of Venus. This *thematic* movement from historical Florence to the eternal garden parallels what has been described here as the *poetics* of the *Stanze*'s mythography: the fitting of historical events—the tournament of 1475—into a poetic typology inherited from literary history. Such a typology may claim to belong to a timeless, divine realm of meaning outside of history (the inspiration myth of the *Nutricia*), but that claim is as much a product of wishful thinking as Venus's hermetically sealed garden. History may turn to poetry for interpretation, but poetry's findings are not definitive, only provisional, waiting for future history to prove them right or wrong. The interpretative movement is necessarily one-way: the attempt to read a traditionally fixed poetic meaning back into history reveals the kind of discontinuity which would, in fact, cut the *Stanze* short. Historical events outstripped the mythmaking of the poem. The death of Simonetta and the assassination of Giuliano caused Poliziano to set aside his pen.[23] Fortune and Death, the historical forces against which the poem pits itself from its opening stanza, will nonetheless have the last word.

Notes

1/ For Poliziano's relations with Ficino, see Arnaldo della Torre, *Storia della Accademia Platonica di Firenze* (Florence: G. Carnesecchi, 1902), pp. 657–58. For the date of Pico's first meeting with Poliziano and their subsequent friendship, see Eugenio Garin, *Giovanni*

Pico della Mirandola: Vita e Dottrina (Florence: Le Monnier, 1937), pp. 5–6, 41 ff.

2/ Giorgio Vasari, *The Lives of the Painters, Sculptors and Architects*, trans. A. B. Hinds (London: L. M. Dent & Sons; New York: E. P. Dutton & Co., 1927), vol. 4,

p. 112. Ascanio Condivi, *Vita di Michelagnolo Buonarotti* (Milan: B.U.R., 1964), pp. 28–29.

3/ *Il Morgante Maggiore* XXVIII, 145–48.

4/ The use of the *Fourth Eclogue* for courtly encomium was a commonplace in *quattrocento* poetry. See

Pulci's eulogy of Lorenzo at the end of the *Morgante* XXVIII, 151, and Matteo Maria Boiardo's *Vasilicomantia* in praise of the Este at Ferrara. For the idea of renewal as a deep-rooted feature of Florentine religious consciousness, see Donald Weinstein, *Savonarola and Florence* (Princeton: Princeton University Press, 1970), pp. 27–66.

5/ German Arciniegas, *Amerigo and the New World*, trans. Harriet de Onis (New York: Alfred A. Knopf, 1955), p. 56.

6/ For Lorenzo and Simonetta, see André Rochon, *La Jeunesse de Laurent de Medicis* (Paris: "Les Belles Lettres," 1963), pp. 246–48.

7/ Francesco De Sanctis, *Storia della letteratura italiana*, ed. Luigi Russo (Milan: Feltrinelli, 1960), vol. 1, p. 369. De Sanctis's criticism plays with the pun on the word *Stanze* which means both "stanzas" and "rooms." While De Sanctis himself valorized form as the aesthetic essence of art, he insisted that poetry possess some link to what he called "reality," a quality he found lacking in the literature of the Renaissance humanists. Hence Poliziano's "rooms," while highly decorative, are empty. The same critical position can be found in De Sanctis's judgment of Ariosto as the greatest Italian literary "artist" as distinguished from "poet" in vol. 2, pp. 64–65.

8/ Benedetto Croce, *Estetica* (Bari: Laterza, 1912), p. 31 ff. Croce edited De Sanctis's *Storia* and accorded a chapter to him in his history of aesthetics. It should be pointed out that Croce understood perfectly well, although with disapproval, the didactic aims of Renaissance writing. See p. 210 ff.

9/ For the Latin text of the letter to Cortese, see *Prosatori Latini del Quattrocento*, ed. Eugenio Garin (Milan: Ricciardi, 1953), pp. 902–4.

10/ For a masterful survey of Poliziano's method in the *Miscellanea*, see A. Grafton, "On the Scholarship of Politian and Its Context," *Journal of the Warburg and Courtauld Institutes* 40 (1977), pp. 150–88.

11/ *Nutricia*, 188–96. For Homer as the first term in the line of poetic inspiration, see Poliziano's *Ambra*, 8–16. For the texts of Poliziano's Latin poetry, see *Prose Volgari Inedite e Poesie Latine e Greche edite e inedite*, ed. Isidoro del Lungo (Florence: Barbera, 1867).

12/ For the role played by poetry and mythology in the thought of the late *quattrocento*, see Eugenio Garin's illuminating chapter, "Le Favole Antiche," in *Medioevo e Rinascimento* (Bari: Laterza, 1966), pp. 66–89.

13/ Professor Sandra Bermann of Princeton University has pointed out to me that Minerva, Glory, and Love may here represent the three parts—intellective, irascible, and appetitive—of the Platonic soul. For an attempt to read the *Stanze* in terms of Neoplatonist erotic doctrine, see the articles of Arnolfo Ferruolo, "A Trend in Renaissance Thought and Art: Poliziano's *Stanze per la Giostra*," *The Romanic Review* 44 (1953), pp. 246–56, and "Botticelli's Mythologies, Ficino's *De Amore*, Poliziano's *Stanze per la Giostra*: Their Circle of Love," *The Art Bulletin* 37 (1955), pp. 16–25.

14/ See especially Guinizelli's *canzone* on love and nobility, *Al cor gentil ripara sempre Amore*, and Dante's first famous *canzone*, *Donne ch'avete intelletto d'amore* in the *Vita Nuova*. Poliziano virtually quotes the opening lines of the Guinizelli poem in Book II, stanza 45.

15/ Dante used the centaur as an emblem of irascibility in the twelfth canto of the *Inferno*, and Botticelli depicted the victory of reason over irascibility in the moral-political allegory of *Pallas and the Centaur* (Uffizi). That Julio, before he encounters and falls in love with Simonetta, personifies the irascible disposition is evidenced by his later identification with Mars. Ficino offers the following explanation of the union of Mars and Venus in his *Commentary on Plotinus (In Librum Quartum de Dubiis Animae Secundum: In Cap. XXVIII): Sunt autem concupiscendi & irascendi vires quasi germanae: nam proclives ad libidinem: sunt etiam propensiores ad iram, atque vicissim, ut non immerito Martem cum Venere poetae coniunxerint.*

For the forces of concupiscence and wrath are almost brother and sister: for those who are inclined to lust may be even more prone to wrath, and vice versa, so that not unjustly did the poets join Mars with Venus. Ficino, *Opera Omnia* (1576; reprint ed., Turin: Bottega d'Erasmo, 1959), vol. 2, ii, p. 1745.

16/ *Marsilio Ficino's Commentary on Plato's Symposium,* trans. Sears Reynolds Jayne, The University of Missouri Studies, vol. 19, no. 1 (Columbia: University of Missouri, 1944), p. 146.

17/ Ibid., p. 202.

18/ For Vulcan as the founder of civilization see Erwin Panovsky, "The Early History of Man in Two Cycles of Paintings by Piero di Cosimo," in Panovsky, *Studies in Iconology* (1939; reprint ed., New York: Harper Torchbooks, 1962), pp. 33–67.

19/ I take issue here with the negative reading of the Mars-Venus conjuction advanced by A. Bartlett Giamatti in *The Earthly Paradise and the Renaissance Epic* (Princeton: Princeton University Press, 1966), pp. 133–34. Professor Giamatti calls attention to the use of the verb "pascendo" (stanza 122) which, he contends, holds pejorative connotations: "for 'pascere' is the verb which refers to the way animals eat." Yet Poliziano is only imitating his Lucretian model (pascit amore avidos inhians in te . . .). Moreover Dante uses the substantive form of the verb in question to describe his gaze into the face of Beatrice: "Chi savesse qual era la pastura/ Del viso mio ne l'aspetto beato" (Whoever knew what was the quality of the feeding of my eyes on her blessed countenance . . .), *Paradiso* XXI, 19–20. Professor Giamatti interprets the passage through the later literary tradition (Tasso, Spenser), but the tradition that precedes the *Stanze* does not seem to support his argument.

20/ *Commentary on Plato's Symposium,* p. 145.

21/ Edgar Wind, *Pagan Mysteries in the Renaissance* (New York: Norton, 1968), p. 133.

22/ Ibid., pp. 154 ff.

23/ The polarities of history and poetry are explored by Eugenio Donato in "Death and History in Poliziano's *Stanze,*" *MLN* 80 (Jan. 1965), pp. 27–40. I am much indebted to Donato's thinking, but he rests his case on the unfinished nature of the poem, which I believe is better attributed to external causes than, as Donato maintains, to the intention of irony on the poet's part.

BOOK ONE

I

Le gloriose pompe e' fieri ludi
della città che 'l freno allenta e stringe
a' magnanimi Toschi, e i regni crudi
di quella dea che 'l terzo ciel dipinge,
e i premi degni alli onorati studi,
la mente audace a celebrar mi spinge,
sí che i gran nomi e i fatti egregi e soli
fortuna o morte o tempo non involi.

II

O bello idio ch'al cor per gli occhi inspiri
dolce disir d'amaro pensier pieno,
e pasciti di pianto e di sospiri,
nudrisci l'alme d'un dolce veleno,
gentil fai divenir ciò che tu miri,
né può star cosa vil drento al tuo seno;
Amor, del quale i' son sempre suggetto,
porgi or la mano al mio basso intelletto.

III

Sostien tu el fascio ch'a me tanto pesa,
reggi la lingua, Amor, reggi la mano;
tu principio, tu fin dell'alta impresa,
tuo fia l'onor, s'io già non prego invano;
di', signor, con che lacci da te presa
fu l'alta mente del baron toscano
piú gioven figlio della etrusca Leda,
che reti furno ordite a tanta preda.

IV

E tu, ben nato Laur, sotto il cui velo
Fiorenza lieta in pace si riposa,
né teme i venti o 'l minacciar del celo
o Giove irato in vista piú crucciosa,
accogli all'ombra del tuo santo stelo
la voce umil, tremante e paurosa;
o causa, o fin di tutte le mie voglie,
che sol vivon d'odor delle tuo foglie.

1

My daring mind urges me to celebrate the glorious pageants and the proud games of the city that bridles and gives rein to the magnanimous Tuscans, the cruel realms of the goddess who adorns the third heaven, and the rewards merited by honorable pursuits; in order that fortune, death, or time may not despoil great names and unique and eminent deeds.

2

O fair god: you who inspire through the eyes unto the heart sweet desire full of bitter thought, you nourish souls with a sweet venom, feeding yourself on tears and sighs, you ennoble whatever you regard, for no baseness can exist within your breast; Love, whose subject I am forever, now lend your hand to my low intellect.

3

Sustain the burden that weighs so much upon me, rule, Love, my tongue and hand; you are the beginning and the end of my lofty endeavor, yours will be the honor if this prayer is not in vain; say, my Lord, with what snares you captured the noble mind of the Tuscan baron, the younger son of the Etruscan Leda, what nets were spread out for so great a prey?

4

And you, well-born Laurel, under whose shelter happy Florence rests in peace, fearing neither winds nor threats of heaven, nor irate Jove in his angriest countenance: receive my humble voice, trembling and fearful, under the shade of your sacred trunk; o cause, o goal of all my desires, which draw life only from the fragrance of your leaves.

1/ *the city . . . Tuscans*: Florence. *the goddess*: Venus.
3/ *the Etruscan Leda*: Lucrezia Tornabuoni, the mother of Lorenzo and Giuliano. Leda, after her union with Zeus, gave birth to the heavenly twins, Castor and Pollux.
4/ *well-born Laurel*: Through the convenient pun on his name, Lorenzo and his propagandists appropriated the Petrarchan emblem of evergreen immortality as a metaphor of political stability. *nor irate Jove*: The mythic nature of the laurel included immunity to lightning.

V

Deh, sarà mai che con piú alte note,
se non contasti al mio volar fortuna,
lo spirto delle membra, che devote
ti fuor da' fati insin già dalla cuna,
risuoni te dai Numidi a Boote,
dagl'Indi al mar che 'l nostro celo imbruna,
e posto il nido in tuo felice ligno,
di roco augel diventi un bianco cigno?

VI

Ma fin ch'all'alta impresa tremo e bramo,
e son tarpati i vanni al mio disio,
lo glorioso tuo fratel cantiamo,
che di nuovo trofeo rende giulio
il chiaro sangue e di secondo ramo:
convien ch'i' sudi in questa polver io.
Or muovi prima tu mie' versi, Amore,
ch'ad alto volo impenni ogni vil core.

VII

E se qua su la fama el ver rimbomba,
che la figlia di Leda, o sacro Achille,
poi che 'l corpo lasciasti intro la tomba,
t'accenda ancor d'amorose faville,
lascia tacere un po' tuo maggior tromba
ch'i' fo squillar per l'italiche ville,
e tempra tu la cetra a nuovi carmi,
mentr'io canto l'amor di Iulio e l'armi.

VIII

Nel vago tempo di sua verde etate,
spargendo ancor pel volto il primo fiore,
né avendo il bel Iulio ancor provate
le dolce acerbe cure che dà Amore,
viveasi lieto in pace e 'n libertate;
talor frenando un gentil corridore,
che gloria fu de' ciciliani armenti,
con esso a correr contendea co' venti:

5

Ah, will it ever come to pass—if Fortune does
not oppose my flight—that the spirit of my limbs
(that even from my cradle were consecrated to
you by the fates) may with loftier strains cause
your name to resound from Numidia to Bootes,
from the Indies to the sea which darkens our
skies? Having nested in your happy branch, shall
I, a croaking bird, turn into a white swan?

6

While I still only yearn and tremble before that
exalted enterprise, and the wings of my desire
are clipped, let us sing of your glorious brother,
who delights his renowned family with a new
trophy, a second branch: this is the dusty arena
where I, too, must sweat. Now be first to move
my verses, Love, you who fledge base hearts for
lofty flight.

7

And, o sacred Achilles, if Fame here on earth
truly reports that the daughter of Leda still
kindles you with amorous sparks after you left
your body inside the tomb, let me leave silent
awhile your greater trumpet that I am causing
to blare through the Italian cities; tune your
lyre for untried songs, while I sing the love
and the arms of Julio.

8

In the lovely time of his green age, the first flower yet blossoming on his cheeks, fair Julio, as
yet inexperienced in the bittersweet cares which
Love provides, lived content in peace and liberty; sometimes bridling a noble steed, the glory
of the Sicilian herds, he would race, contending
with the winds:

5/ *from Numidia to Bootes
. . . our skies*: From south to
north, from east to west.
Bootes, the ploughman, is a
northern constellation.
6/ *a second branch*: The palm
branch, the ancient reward
for military prowess. (See I,
83.) Giuliano's victory in
1475 was the second for the
Medici family; Lorenzo had
sponsored and won the tournament of 1469.
7/ *the daughter of Leda*:
Helen of Troy. According to
Hellenistic mythographers
(Lycophron, *Alexandra*, 169–
79; the *New History* of Ptol-
emaeus Hephaestionis cited
by Photius in the *Bibliotheca*,
cod. 190), the shades of Achilles and Helen were married
while they enjoyed the blessings of the afterlife upon the
Fortunate Isles. *your greater
trumpet*: Poliziano alludes to
his unfinished translation of
the *Iliad*.

IX

ora a guisa saltar di leopardo,
or destro fea rotarlo in breve giro;
or fea ronzar per l'aere un lento dardo,
dando sovente a fere agro martiro.
Cotal viveasi il giovene gagliardo;
né pensando al suo fato acerbo e diro,
né certo ancor de' suo' futuri pianti,
solea gabbarsi delli afflitti amanti.

X

Ah quante ninfe per lui sospirorno!
Ma fu sí altero sempre il giovinetto,
che mai le ninfe amanti nol piegorno,
mai poté riscaldarsi il freddo petto.
Facea sovente pe' boschi soggiorno,
inculto sempre e rigido in aspetto;
e 'l volto difendea dal solar raggio,
con ghirlanda di pino o verde faggio.

XI

Poi, quando già nel ciel parean le stelle,
tutto gioioso a sua magion tornava;
e 'n compagnia delle nove sorelle
celesti versi con disio cantava,
e d'antica virtú mille fiammelle
con gli alti carmi ne' petti destava:
cosí, chiamando amor lascivia umana,
si godea con le Muse o con Diana.

XII

E se talor nel ceco labirinto
errar vedeva un miserello amante,
di dolor carco, di pietà dipinto,
seguir della nemica sua le piante,
e dove Amor il cor li avessi avinto,
lí pascer l'alma di dua luci sante
preso nelle amorose crudel gogne,
sí l'assaliva con agre rampogne:

9
now, with skill, causing him to bound like a
leopard, now compelling him to turn in a narrow
circle, now making a pliant spear whistle through
the air, often dealing bitter death to the wild
game. So the gallant youth used to live; with no
thought for his own harsh and dire fate, as yet
unaware of his tears to come, he would make
fun of stricken lovers.

10
How many nymphs sighed for him! But the amorous nymphs could never make the arrogant
boy yield, nor could his cold breast be warmed.
He often made his home in the forest, always
unkempt and hardened in aspect; he protected
his face from the rays of the sun with a garland
of pine or green beech.

11
Then, once the stars had appeared in the sky, he
would happily return to his house; in the company of the nine sisters he would longingly sing
celestial verses, and with his noble poetry he
would awaken a thousand flames of ancient virtue in the breasts of his listeners: and thus, calling love nothing but human lust, he rejoiced
with the Muses or with Diana.

12
And if sometime he should see a miserable lover,
laden with grief and the picture of woe, wander
in the sightless labyrinth, following the footsteps
of his enemy, feeding his soul upon two saintly
eyes wherein Love had bound his heart, held in
the cruel amorous fetters, Julio would assail him
with bitter reproach:

XIII

«Scuoti, meschin, del petto il ceco errore,
ch'a te stessi te fura, ad altrui porge;
non nudrir di lusinghe un van furore,
che di pigra lascivia e d'ozio sorge.
Costui che 'l vulgo errante chiama Amore
è dolce insania a chi piú acuto scorge:
sí bel titol d'Amore ha dato il mondo
a una ceca peste, a un mal giocondo.

XIV

Ah quanto è uom meschin, che cangia voglia
per donna, o mai per lei s'allegra o dole;
e qual per lei di libertà si spoglia
o crede a sui sembianti, a sue parole!
Ché sempre è piú leggier ch'al vento foglia,
e mille volte el dí vuole e disvuole:
segue chi fugge, a chi la vuol s'asconde,
e vanne e vien, come alla riva l'onde.

XV

Giovane donna sembra veramente
quasi sotto un bel mare acuto scoglio,
o ver tra' fiori un giovincel serpente
uscito pur mo' fuor del vecchio scoglio.
Ah quanto è fra' piú miseri dolente
chi può soffrir di donna il fero orgoglio!
Ché quanto ha il volto piú di biltà pieno,
piú cela inganni nel fallace seno.

XVI

Con essi gli occhi giovenili invesca
Amor, ch'ogni pensier maschio vi fura;
e quale un tratto ingoza la dolce esca
mai di sua propria libertà non cura;
ma, come se pur Lete Amor vi mesca,
tosto obliate vostra alta natura;
né poi viril pensiero in voi germoglia,
sí del proprio valor costui vi spoglia.

13

"Wretch, shake from your breast that blind error that robs you of yourself and delivers you to another; do not nourish with flattery a vain frenzy that rises from indolent lust and sloth. He whom the erring common folk call Love is, when more clearly perceived, a sweet madness: the world has given that beautiful name of Love to an unseen plague, to a gladsome evil.

14

"Ah, how miserable is the man who changes his mind for a woman or ever becomes happy or sad on her account! who strips himself of liberty for her, or believes in her looks and words! For she is ever flightier than a windswept leaf, and she wishes and unwishes a thousand times a day: she pursues the man who flees, hides from one who desires her, she comes and goes like waves upon the shore.

15

"Truly a young woman resembles a sharp reef beneath a fair sea, or among flowers a young serpent that has just now issued from its sloughed-off skin. Most sorrowful wretch is he who endures a woman's fierce pride! The more her face is full of beauty, the more deceptions she hides in her false breast.

16

"With these Love, who steals away your every masculine thought, lime-snares youthful eyes; whoever once swallows the sweet bait cares no more for his own freedom; rather, as if Love poured Lethe in your cup, you soon forget your higher nature; no manly thought may grow in you: he so strips you of your proper valor.

XVII

Quanto è piú dolce, quanto è piú securo
seguir le fere fugitive in caccia
fra boschi antichi fuor di fossa o muro,
e spiar lor covil per lunga traccia!
Veder la valle e 'l colle e l'aer piú puro,
l'erbe e' fior, l'acqua viva chiara e ghiaccia!
Udir li augei svernar, rimbombar l'onde,
e dolce al vento mormorar le fronde!

XVIII

Quanto giova a mirar pender da un'erta
le capre, e pascer questo e quel virgulto;
e 'l montanaro all'ombra piú conserta
destar la sua zampogna e 'l verso inculto;
veder la terra di pomi coperta,
ogni arbor da' suoi frutti quasi occulto;
veder cozzar monton, vacche mughiare
e le biade ondeggiar come fa il mare!

XIX

Or delle pecorelle il rozo mastro
si vede alla sua torma aprir la sbarra;
poi quando muove lor con suo vincastro,
dolce è a notar come a ciascuna garra.
Or si vede il villan domar col rastro
le dure zolle, or maneggiar la marra;
or la contadinella scinta e scalza
star coll'oche a filar sotto una balza.

XX

In cotal guisa già l'antiche genti
si crede esser godute al secol d'oro;
né fatte ancor le madre eron dolenti
de' morti figli al marzial lavoro;
né si credeva ancor la vita a' venti,
né del giogo doleasi ancora il toro;
lor case eron fronzute querce e grande,
ch'avean nel tronco mèl, ne' rami ghiande.

17

"How much sweeter, how much safer to hunt
the fleeing beasts through ancient forests outside
of wall or moat, to discover their dens after long
tracking! To see the valleys, and hills, and the
purer air, the grass and flowers, the clear icy living waters! To hear the birds unwinter themselves, the cascades resounding, the sweet mur-
mur of branches in the wind!

18

"How pleasing to see goats cling to the cliffs and
feed on this bush and that; and the mountain
shepherd in the densest shade awaken his reed-
pipe and uncultured verse; to see the earth covered with fruit, every tree almost hidden by its
yield; to see rams locking horns, cattle lowing,
grain fields waving like the sea!

19

"Now the rude master of the sheep is seen to
open the gate for his flocks; when he prods them
with his crook, it is delightful to note how he
chides each one. Now the rustic tames the hard
clods with his rake, now he wields his hoe; now,
beneath a rocky ledge, the ungirded, barefoot
peasant girl stays to spin beside her geese.

20

"In this manner, the oldest folk are believed to
have enjoyed the golden age; mothers were not
yet made sorrowful by sons killed in martial endeavor; human life was not yet entrusted to the
winds; the bull did not yet complain of the
yoke; their houses were great leafy oaks that
possessed honey in their trunks and acorns on
their boughs.

XXI

Non era ancor la scelerata sete
del crudele oro entrata nel bel mondo;
viveansi in libertà le genti liete,
e non solcato il campo era fecondo.
Fortuna invidiosa a lor quiete
ruppe ogni legge, e pietà misse in fondo;
lussuria entrò ne' petti e quel furore
che la meschina gente chiama amore.»

XXII

In cotal guisa rimordea sovente
l'altero giovinetto e sacri amanti,
come talor chi sé gioioso sente
non sa ben porger fede alli altrui pianti;
ma qualche miserello, a cui l'ardente
fiamme struggeano i nervi tutti quanti,
gridava al ciel: «Giusto sdegno ti muova,
Amor, che costui creda almen per pruova.»

XXIII

Né fu Cupido sordo al pio lamento,
e 'ncominciò crudelmente ridendo:
"Dunque non sono idio? dunque è già spento
mie foco con che il mondo tutto accendo?
Io pur fei Giove mughiar fra l'armento,
io Febo drieto a Dafne gir piangendo,
io trassi Pluto delle infernal segge:
e che non ubidisce alla mia legge?

XXIV

Io fo cadere al tigre la sua rabbia,
al leone il fer rughio, al drago il fischio;
e quale è uom di sí secura labbia,
che fuggir possa il mio tenace vischio?
Or, ch'un superbo in sí vil pregio m'abbia
che di non esser dio vegna a gran rischio?
Or veggiàn se 'l meschin ch'Amor riprende,
da dua begli occhi se stesso or difende."

21

"The evil thirst for cruel gold had not yet entered the beautiful world; the happy people lived
in liberty, the fields, though unplowed, were
plentiful. Fortune, envious of their peace, broke
all laws and overthrew piety; lust entered human
hearts and that madness which the people, in
their misery, call love."

22

In this manner the haughty youth would often
reprove Cupid's consecrated lovers, as one, who,
joyous himself, cannot put faith in the tears of
others; but one poor wretch whose sinews were
being consumed by ardent flames cried out to
heaven: "Let just disdain move you, Love, let
him at least believe by experience!"

23

Cupid was not deaf to the pious complaint;
laughing cruelly, he began: "Am I not then a
god? is my fire with which I burn the entire
world already spent? Indeed, I made Jove bellow among the herd, I caused Phoebus to run
weeping after Daphne, I drew Pluto from his
infernal seat: and what creature does not obey
my law?

24

"I cause the tiger to lose its rage, the dragon its
hiss, the lion its savage roar; and what man, out-
wardly so secure, can escape my tenacious lime?
Is my godhood now jeopardized because one
proud man holds me in such low esteem? Let us
see whether the wretch who reproaches Love
can now defend himself from two fair eyes."

23/ *Jove bellow*: Enamored
of Europa, Jupiter trans-
formed himself into a bull.
I drew Pluto . . . seat: Pluto
left his underworld kingdom
to carry off Proserpina.

XXV

Zefiro già, di be' fioretti adorno,
avea de' monti tolta ogni pruina;
avea fatto al suo nido già ritorno
la stanca rondinella peregrina;
risonava la selva intorno intorno
soavemente all'òra mattutina,
e la ingegnosa pecchia al primo albore
giva predando ora uno or altro fiore.

XXVI

L'ardito Iulio, al giorno ancora acerbo,
allor ch'al tufo torna la civetta,
fatto frenare il corridor superbo,
verso la selva con sua gente eletta
prese el cammino, e sotto buon riserbo
seguial de' fedel can la schiera stretta;
di ciò che fa mestieri a caccia adorni,
con archi e lacci e spiedi e dardi e corni.

XXVII

Già circundata avea la lieta schiera
il folto bosco, e già con grave orrore
del suo covil si destava ogni fera;
givan seguendo e bracchi il lungo odore;
ogni varco da lacci e can chiuso era,
di stormir d'abbaiar cresce il romore,
di fischi e bussi tutto il bosco suona,
del rimbombar de' corni el cel rintruona.

XXVIII

Con tal romor, qualor piú l'aer discorda,
di Giove il foco d'alta nube piomba;
con tal tumulto, onde la gente assorda,
dall'alte cataratte il Nil rimbomba;
con tale orror, del latin sangue ingorda,
sonò Megera la tartarea tromba.
Qual animal di stiza par si roda,
qual serra al ventre la tremante coda.

25

Zephyr, adorned with lovely flowers, had already lifted the hoarfrost from the mountains;
the weary pilgrim swallow had already returned
to its nest; all about the forest resounded sweetly in the morning breeze, and the ingenious bee
preyed upon blossom after blossom in the first
light of dawn.

26

When morning was still dark, at the time that
the owl was returning to its tuff, daring Julio,
having ordered his proud courser to be bridled,
made his way toward the forest beside his chos-
en company (and the close band of faithful
hounds followed under just restraint); equipped
with what was useful for the hunt: bows and
snares and spears and darts and horns.

27

The happy band had already circled the thick
woods; and now each beast awakened with great
terror in its den; the hounds followed the drawn-
out scent; every path was closed by dog and
snare. The noise of rustling and barking grows,
all the forest resounds with whistles and blows,
the heavens thunder with the echoing of horns.

28

With like report, when the air falls into discord,
the fire of Jove crashes from a lofty cloud; with
such tumult, from which neighboring folk grow
deaf, the Nile thunders from its high cataracts;
with such horror, Megaera, gluttonous for Latin
blood, sounded the Tartarean trumpet. One
beast appeared to gnaw itself in rage, another
pressed its trembling tail between its legs.

28/ *Megaera*: One of the
Furies.

XXIX

Spargesi tutta la bella compagna:
altri alle reti, altri alla via piú stretta;
chi serba in coppia e can, chi gli scompagna;
chi già 'l suo ammette, chi 'l richiama e alletta;
chi sprona el buon destrier per la campagna;
chi l'adirata fera armato aspetta;
chi si sta sovra un ramo a buon riguardo,
chi in man lo spiede e chi s'acconcia el dardo.

XXX

Già le setole arriccia e arruota e denti
el porco entro 'l burron; già d'una grotta
spunta giú 'l cavriuol; già e vecchi armenti
de' cervi van pel pian fuggendo in frotta;
timor gl'inganni della volpe ha spenti;
le lepri al primo assalto vanno in rotta;
di sua tana stordita esce ogni belva;
l'astuto lupo vie piú si rinselva,

XXXI

e rinselvato le sagace nare
del picciol bracco pur teme il meschino;
ma 'l cervio par del veltro paventare,
de' lacci el porco o del fero mastino.
Vedesi lieto or qua or là volare
fuor d'ogni schiera il giovan peregrino;
pel folto bosco el fer caval mette ale,
e trista fa qual fera Iulio assale.

XXXII

Qual el centaur per la nevosa selva
di Pelio o d'Emo va feroce in caccia,
dalle lor tane predando ogni belva:
or l'orso uccide, or al lion minaccia;
quanto è piú ardita fera piú s'inselva,
e 'l sangue a tutte drento al cor s'aghiaccia;
la selva trema e gli cede ogni pianta,
gli arbori abbatte o sveglie, o rami schianta.

29

The fair company scatters: some to the nets,
some to the narrowest path; one holds together
a brace of hounds, another uncouples, a third
unleashes, still another lures and recalls them;
one spurs his excellent steed through the fields;
one, armed, awaits the enraged beast; one remains vigilant upon a branch, one readies his
spear in his hand, another his dart.

30

Now the boar raises its bristles and gnashes its
teeth in the ravine; now the roebuck appears
from a cave; now the ancient herds of deer flee
in a troop across the plain; fear has extinguished
the cunning of the fox; the hares are routed by
the first assault; every beast leaves its den, be-
wildered; the astute wolf retreats further within
the woods,

31

and once in the woods, the wretch still fears the
little hound's expert nostrils; but the stag seems
to tremble at the greyhound, the boar at the
snares or the fierce mastiff. Joyful, unaccompa-
nied, the extraordinary youth seems to fly, now
here, now there; his spirited steed takes wing
through the thick forest; unfortunate the beast
that Julio assails.

32

In such a way, the ferocious Centaur goes to
hunt through the snowy forests of Pelion or
Haemus, chasing every beast from its den: now
he kills the bear, now menaces the lion; the braver the beast the further within the woods it
hides, blood turns to ice inside each heart; the
woods tremble, and every plant gives way, he
beats down or uproots the trees, or shatters
their branches.

32/ *Pelion or Haemus*: Mt.
Pelion is in Thessaly; the Hae-
mus range, now called the
Great Balkan, lies in Thrace.

XXXIII

Ah quanto a mirar Iulio è fera cosa
romper la via dove piú 'l bosco è folto
per trar di macchia la bestia crucciosa,
con verde ramo intorno al capo avolto,
colla chioma arruffata e polverosa,
e d'onesto sudor bagnato il volto!
Ivi consiglio a sua fera vendetta
prese Amor, che ben loco e tempo aspetta;

XXXIV

e con sua man di leve aier compuose
l'imagin d'una cervia altera e bella:
con alta fronte, con corna ramose,
candida tutta, leggiadretta e snella.
E come tra le fere paventose
al gioven cacciator s'offerse quella,
lieto spronò il destrier per lei seguire,
pensando in brieve darli agro martire.

XXXV

Ma poi che 'nvan dal braccio el dardo scosse,
del foder trasse fuor la fida spada,
e con tanto furor il corsier mosse,
che 'l bosco folto sembrava ampia strada.
La bella fera, come stanca fosse,
piú lenta tuttavia par che sen vada;
ma quando par che già la stringa o tocchi,
picciol campo riprende avanti alli occhi.

XXXVI

Quanto piú segue invan la vana effigie,
tanto piú di seguirla invan s'accende;
tuttavia preme sue stanche vestigie,
sempre la giunge, e pur mai non la prende:
qual fino al labro sta nelle onde stigie
Tantalo, e 'l bel giardin vicin gli pende,
ma qualor l'acqua o il pome vuol gustare,
subito l'acqua e 'l pome via dispare.

33

How fierce a thing it is to see Julio! With green
garland encircling his head, with dusty and ruf-
fled hair, and face bathed with honest sweat, he
breaks through where the woods are thickest to
draw the angry beast out of the brush. There
Love, who waits the right time and place, took
counsel for his vengeance;

34

And with his hands he created out of light air
the image of a haughty and beautiful doe: lofty
forehead, branching horns, completely white,
light and slender. And as from among the frightened beasts she offered herself to the young
hunter, he joyfully spurred his steed in pursuit,
thinking shortly to give her bitter torment.

35

But after he had cast his dart in vain, he drew
his faithful sword out of its sheath, and urged
his charger with such furor that the dense woods
seemed an open road. The beautiful creature appears to slow down as if she were weary, but just
when it seems that he will reach or touch her,
she regains a little ground before his eyes.

36

The more he pursues in vain the vain image, the
more he burns in vain to pursue it; he presses
ever and ever upon her tired tracks, he draws
ever nearer but never overtakes her: just so Tan-
talus stands up to his lips in the Stygian waters
and the fair orchard hangs down nearby, but
whenever he wishes to taste water or fruit, they
instantly disappear.

XXXVII

Era già drieto alla sua desianza
gran tratta da' compagni allontanato,
né pur d'un passo ancor la preda avanza,
e già tutto el destrier sente affannato;
ma pur seguendo sua vana speranza,
pervenne in un fiorito e verde prato:
ivi sotto un vel candido li apparve
lieta una ninfa, e via la fera sparve.

XXXVIII

La fera sparve via dalle suo ciglia,
ma 'l gioven della fera omai non cura;
anzi ristringe al corridor la briglia,
e lo raffrena sovra alla verdura.
Ivi tutto ripien di maraviglia
pur della ninfa mira la figura:
parli che dal bel viso e da' begli occhi
una nuova dolcezza al cor gli fiocchi.

XXXIX

Qual tigre, a cui dalla pietrosa tana
ha tolto il cacciator li suoi car figli,
rabbiosa il segue per la selva ircana,
che tosto crede insanguinar gli artigli;
poi resta d'uno specchio all'ombra vana,
all'ombra ch'e suoi nati par somigli;
e mentre di tal vista s'innamora
la sciocca, el predator la via divora.

XL

Tosto Cupido entro a' begli occhi ascoso,
al nervo adatta del suo stral la cocca,
poi tira quel col braccio poderoso,
tal che raggiugne e l'una e l'altra cocca;
la man sinistra con l'oro focoso
la destra poppa colla corda tocca:
né pria per l'aer ronzando esce 'l quadrello,
che Iulio drento al cor sentito ha quello.

37
In pursuit of his desire, Julio had by now sepa-
rated himself a great distance from his companions, but he still had not gained a step on his
prey, and his horse was already exhausted; but,
still following his vain hope, he came upon a
green and flowery meadow: here, veiled in white,
a lovely nymph appeared before him, and the
doe vanished away.

38
The animal vanished from his sight. But now the
youth scarcely cares about the deer; rather he
tugs the bridle of his courser, and reins him in
upon the greensward. Here, filled with wonder,
he gazes upon the features of the nymph: it
seems to him that from her lovely face and eyes
a new sweetness showers into his heart.

39
Even so an enraged tigress, from whose rocky
den a hunter has stolen her cherished young, follows him through the Hyrcanian woods, thinking soon to bloody her claws; then pauses before
the vain reflection of a mirroring water, before
the reflection that resembles her children; and
while the fool is enamored of that sight, the
hunter flies away.

40
Quickly, Cupid, hidden in those beautiful eyes,
adjusts the notch of his arrow to his bowstring,
then he draws back with his powerful arm so
that the two ends of the bow meet; his left
hand is touched by the point of fiery gold, his
right breast by the string: the arrow does not be-
gin to hiss through the air before Julio has felt
it inside his heart.

39/ *Hyrcanian*: The region of
Hyrcania lies on the southeast
coast of the Caspian Sea.

XLI

Ahi qual divenne! ah come al giovinetto
corse il gran foco in tutte le midolle!
che tremito gli scosse il cor nel petto!
d'un ghiacciato sudor tutto era molle;
e fatto ghiotto del suo dolce aspetto,
giammai li occhi da li occhi levar puolle;
ma tutto preso dal vago splendore,
non s'accorge el meschin che quivi è Amore.

XLII

Non s'accorge ch'Amor lí drento è armato
per sol turbar la suo lunga quiete;
non s'accorge a che nodo è già legato,
non conosce suo piaghe ancor segrete;
di piacer, di disir tutto è invescato,
e cosí il cacciator preso è alla rete.
Le braccia fra sé loda e 'l viso e 'l crino,
e 'n lei discerne un non so che divino.

XLIII

Candida è ella, e candida la vesta,
ma pur di rose e fior dipinta e d'erba;
lo inanellato crin dall'aurea testa
scende in la fronte umilmente superba.
Rideli a torno tutta la foresta,
e quanto può suo cure disacerba;
nell'atto regalmente è mansueta,
e pur col ciglio le tempeste acqueta.

XLIV

Folgoron gli occhi d'un dolce sereno,
ove sue face tien Cupido ascose;
l'aier d'intorno si fa tutto ameno
ovunque gira le luce amorose.
Di celeste letizia il volto ha pieno,
dolce dipinto di ligustri e rose;
ogni aura tace al suo parlar divino,
e canta ogni augelletto in suo latino.

41

Ah, what a change came over him! Ah, how the
fire rushed all through the young man's marrow!
What a trembling shook the heart within his
breast! He was soaked with an icy sweat; made
avid for her sweet face, not once can he remove
his eyes from hers; utterly captured by their
charming splendor, the wretch does not perceive that therein is Love.

42

He does not perceive that Love therein is armed
solely to disturb his long peace; he does not perceive the knot by which he is already tied, he
does not recognize his still secret wounds: he is
lime-snared entirely by pleasure and desire, and
thus the hunter is taken in the net. He inwardly
praises her arms, her face, and her hair, and in
her he discerns something divine.

43

She is fair-skinned, unblemished white, and
white is her garment, though ornamented with
roses, flowers, and grass; the ringlets of her gold-
en hair descend on a forehead humbly proud.
The whole forest smiles about her, and, as it
may, lightens her cares; in her movement she is
regally mild, her glance alone could quiet a tem-
pest.

44

From her eyes there flashes a honeyed calm in
which Cupid hides his torch; wherever she turns
those amorous eyes, the air about her becomes
serene. Her face, sweetly painted with privet and
roses, is filled with heavenly joy; every breeze is
hushed before her divine speech, and every little
bird sings out in its own language.

XLV
Con lei sen va Onestate umile e piana
che d'ogni chiuso cor volge la chiave;
con lei va Gentilezza in vista umana,
e da lei impara il dolce andar soave.
Non può mirarli il viso alma villana,
se pria di suo fallir doglia non have;
tanti cori Amor piglia fere o ancide,
quanto ella o dolce parla o dolce ride.

XLVI
Sembra Talia se in man prende la cetra,
sembra Minerva se in man prende l'asta;
se l'arco ha in mano, al fianco la faretra,
giurar potrai che sia Diana casta.
Ira dal volto suo trista s'arretra,
e poco, avanti a lei, Superbia basta;
ogni dolce virtú l'è in compagnia,
Biltà la mostra a dito e Leggiadria.

XLVII
Ell'era assisa sovra la verdura,
allegra, e ghirlandetta avea contesta
di quanti fior creassi mai natura,
de' quai tutta dipinta era sua vesta.
E come prima al gioven puose cura,
alquanto paurosa alzò la testa;
poi colla bianca man ripreso il lembo,
levossi in piè con di fior pieno un grembo.

XLVIII
Già s'inviava, per quindi partire,
la ninfa sovra l'erba, lenta lenta,
lasciando il giovinetto in gran martire,
che fuor di lei null'altro omai talenta.
Ma non possendo el miser ciò soffrire,
con qualche priego d'arrestarla tenta;
per che, tutto tremando e tutto ardendo,
cosí umilmente incominciò dicendo:

Beside her goes humble, gentle Chastity, who
turns the key to every locked heart; with her
goes Nobility with kindly appearance and imitates her sweet graceful step. No base soul can
regard her face without first repenting of its
faults; Love captures, wounds, and kills all those
hearts with whom she sweetly speaks or sweetly
laughs.

46
She would resemble Thalia if she took lyre in
hand, Minerva, if she held a spear; if she had a
bow in hand and quiver at her side, you would
swear she was chaste Diana. Anger, grieving,
withdraws from before her countenance, Pride
avails little in her presence; every sweet virtue is
in her company, Beauty and Grace point her out.

47
She was seated upon the grass, and, lighthearted,
had woven a garland out of as many flowers as
nature ever created, the flowers with which her
garment was decorated. As first she noticed the
youth, she somewhat timidly raised her head;
then having gathered up the hem of her skirt
with her white hand, she rose to her feet, her lap
filled with flowers.

48
Now the nymph was slowly making her way
across the grass, leaving the youth in great pain,
for he desired nothing else but her. The wretch,
unable to endure her parting, sought to stay her
with some plea; whereupon, all trembling and
burning, he humbly began to speak:

46/ *Thalia*: The Muse of
Comedy.

XLIX

«O qual che tu ti sia, vergin sovrana,
o ninfa o dea, ma dea m'assembri certo;
se dea, forse se' tu la mia Diana;
se pur mortal, chi tu sia fammi certo,
ché tua sembianza è fuor di guisa umana;
né so già io qual sia tanto mio merto,
qual dal cel grazia, qual sí amica stella,
ch'io degno sia veder cosa sí bella.»

L

Volta la ninfa al suon delle parole,
lampeggiò d'un sí dolce e vago riso,
che i monti avre' fatto ir, restare il sole:
ché ben parve s'aprissi un paradiso.
Poi formò voce fra perle e viole,
tal ch'un marmo per mezo avre' diviso;
soave, saggia e di dolceza piena,
da innamorar non ch'altri una Sirena:

LI

«Io non son qual tua mente invano auguria,
non d'altar degna, non di pura vittima;
ma là sovra Arno innella vostra Etruria
sto soggiogata alla teda legittima;
mia natal patria è nella aspra Liguria,
sovra una costa alla riva marittima,
ove fuor de' gran massi indarno gemere
si sente il fer Nettunno e irato fremere.

LII

Sovente in questo loco mi diporto,
qui vegno a soggiornar tutta soletta;
questo è de' mia pensieri un dolce porto,
qui l'erba e' fior, qui il fresco aier m'alletta;
quinci il tornare a mia magione è accorto,
qui lieta mi dimoro Simonetta,
all'ombre, a qualche chiara e fresca linfa,
e spesso in compagnia d'alcuna ninfa.

"Whatever you are, o sovereign virgin, nymph or
goddess, but certainly you seem a goddess to
me; if a goddess, perhaps you are my Diana; if
mortal, tell me who you are, for your appearance surpasses human nature; nor do I yet know
what merit of mine, what grace from heaven,
what friendly star makes me worthy to see
anything so beautiful."

50

The nymph turned at the sound of his words,
she flashed a smile so sweet and lovely that it
might have moved mountains or stopped the
sun; for indeed it seemed as if a paradise were
opening. Then, between pearls and violets, she
formed words that might have split marble; so
soft, wise, and full of sweetness, as might have
enamored even a Siren.

51

"I am not what your mind vainly augurs, not
worthy of an altar nor of a pure sacrifice; but I
live upon the Arno in your Etruria, subject to
the legal bond; my native country is in rugged
Liguria, upon a coastline on the maritime shore,
where, outside the great rock masses, proud and
angry Neptune is heard to shudder and groan in
vain.

52

"I often walk in this place, I come here to so-
journ alone; this is a sweet haven for my
thoughts; here the grass and flowers, here the
fresh air attract me; the return from here to my
house is short; here, I, Simonetta, rest happily in
the shade beside some cool and limpid stream,
often in the company of some other nymph.

51/ *the legal bond*: Marriage.

LIII

Io soglio pur nelli ociosi tempi,
quando nostra fatica s'interrompe,
venire a' sacri altar ne' vostri tempî
fra l'altre donne con l'usate pompe;
ma perch'io in tutto el gran desir t'adempi
e 'l dubio tolga che tuo mente rompe,
meraviglia di mie bellezze tenere
non prender già, ch'io nacqui in grembo a Venere.

LIV

Or poi che 'l sol sue rote in basso cala,
e da questi arbor cade maggior l'ombra,
già cede al grillo la stanca cicala,
già 'l rozo zappator del campo sgombra,
e già dell'alte ville il fumo essala,
la villanella all'uom suo el desco ingombra;
omai riprenderò mia via piú accorta,
e tu lieto ritorna alla tua scorta.»

LV

Poi con occhi piú lieti e piú ridenti,
tal che 'l ciel tutto asserenò d'intorno,
mosse sovra l'erbetta e passi lenti
con atto d'amorosa grazia adorno.
Feciono e boschi allor dolci lamenti
e gli augelletti a pianger cominciorno;
ma l'erba verde sotto i dolci passi
bianca, gialla, vermiglia e azurra fassi.

LVI

Che de' far Iulio? Ahimè, ch'e' pur desidera
seguir sua stella e pur temenza il tiene:
sta come un forsennato, e 'l cor gli assidera,
e gli s'aghiaccia el sangue entro le vene;
sta come un marmo fisso, e pur considera
lei che sen va né pensa di sue pene,
fra sé lodando il dolce andar celeste
e 'l ventilar dell'angelica veste.

53

"In the leisurely holidays, when our work is suspended, I am accustomed, with the usual ceremonies, to go among the other women to the sacred altars of your temples; but in order to satisfy in full your great desire, to remove the doubt that disturbs your mind, do not marvel at my young beauty, for I was born in the lap of Venus.

54

"Now that the sun bends down its chariot wheels, and the shade stretches farther from these trees, the tired cicada already yields to the cricket, already the rustic spadesman leaves the field, and now smoke rises from the farmers' roofs, while the countrywoman loads the table for her man; now I will take my shortest way home, and you may joyfully return to your companions."

55

Then with happier laughing eyes, such that the sky grew fair around her, she slowly moved her steps over the grass, an action adorned with amorous grace. Then the woods made sweet lament, the birds began to weep; but the green grass beneath her sweet steps flowered white, yellow, red, and blue.

56

What should Julio do? Alas, he still desires to follow his star, yet fear holds him back: he stands like a man out of his senses, his heart is chilled, his blood turns to ice inside his veins; he stands like fixed marble, and still he watches her as she departs unaware of his pains, he praises to himself the sweet celestial manner of her walk and the way the wind catches her angelic dress.

53/ *lap of Venus*: Carducci suggests a possible reference to Portovenere ("harbor of Venus"), a town near Genoa. Sapegno sees an allusion to Genoa itself, located on the sea from whose foam the goddess was born.

LVII

E' par che 'l cor del petto se li schianti,
e che del corpo l'alma via si fugga,
e ch'a guisa di brina, al sol davanti,
in pianto tutto si consumi e strugga.
Già si sente esser un degli altri amanti,
e pargli ch'ogni vena Amor li sugga;
or teme di seguirla, or pure agogna,
qui 'l tira Amor, quinci il ritrae vergogna.

LVIII

«U' sono or, Iulio, le sentenze gravi,
la parole magnifiche e' precetti
con che i miseri amanti molestavi?
Perché pur di cacciar non ti diletti?
Or ecco ch'una donna ha in man le chiavi
d'ogni tua voglia, e tutti in sé ristretti
tien, miserello, i tuoi dolci pensieri;
vedi chi tu se' or, chi pur dianzi eri.

LIX

Dianzi eri d'una fera cacciatore,
piú bella fera or t'ha ne' lacci involto;
dianzi eri tuo, or se' fatto d'Amore,
sei or legato, e dianzi eri disciolto.
Dov'è tuo libertà, dov'è 'l tuo core?
Amore e una donna te l'ha tolto.
Ahi, come poco a sé creder uom degge!
ch'a virtute e fortuna Amor pon legge.»

LX

La notte che le cose ci nasconde
tornava ombrata di stellato ammanto,
e' l'usignuol sotto l'amate fronde
cantando ripetea l'antico pianto;
ma sola a' sua lamenti Ecco risponde,
ch'ogni altro augel quetato avea già 'l canto;
dalla chimmeria valle uscian le torme
de' Sogni negri con diverse forme.

And it seems to him that his heart is being torn
from his breast, and that his soul is fleeing his
body, and that, like a frost before the sun, he is
melting and being consumed in tears. Already he
feels himself one among the other lovers, and it
seems to him that Love drinks from all his veins;
now he fears, now he still longs to follow her;
Love draws him one way, shame withdraws him
another.

58

Where now, Julio, are your grave pronounce-
ments, the magnificent words and the precepts
with which you used to offend miserable lovers?
Why don't you enjoy the hunt? Behold now,
wretch, a woman holds all the keys to your desires, and confines all your sweet thoughts to her;
mark who you are now, and who you were before.

59

Before you were the hunter of a wild creature;
now a more beautiful creature has entangled you
in her snares; before you were your own man,
now you belong to Love, now you are bound,
before you were unfettered. Where is your liberty? where is your heart? Love and a woman
have taken them from you. Alas, how little must
man trust to himself! for Love imposes laws on
virtue and fortune.

60

Night that hides the world from us was returning, covered by a starry mantle, and the nightingale, singing under her beloved branches,
repeated her old lament; but only Echo answered
her weeping, for by now every other bird had
stilled its song: the swarms of black Dreams
came out of the Cimmerian valley in their different forms.

60/ *Cimmerian valley*: The
underworld. According to
Homer (*Odyssey* XI, 14 ff.),
the sunless, mist-shrouded
city of the Cimmerians lay on
the river Ocean at the edge of
the world. There Ulysses con-
sulted the shades of Hades.

LXI
E gioven che restati nel bosco erono,
vedendo il cel già le sue stelle accendere,
sentito il segno, al cacciar posa ferono;
ciascun s'affretta a lacci e reti stendere,
poi colla preda in un sentier si schierono:
ivi s'attende sol parole a vendere,
ivi menzogne a vil pregio si mercono;
poi tutti del bel Iulio fra sé cercono.

LXII
Ma non veggendo il car compagno intorno,
ghiacciossi ognun di subita paura
che qualche cruda fera il suo ritorno
non li 'mpedisca o altra ria sciagura.
Chi mostra fuochi, chi squilla el suo corno,
chi forte il chiama per la selva oscura;
le lunghe voci ripercosse abondono,
e «Iulio Iulio» le valli rispondono.

LXIII
Ciascun si sta per la paura incerto
gelato tutto, se non ch'ei pur chiama;
veggiono il cel di tenebre coperto,
né san dove cercar, bench'ognun brama.
Pur «Iulio Iulio» suona il gran diserto;
non sa che farsi omai la gente grama.
Ma poi che molta notte indarno spesono,
dolenti per tornarsi il cammin presono.

LXIV
Cheti sen vanno, e pure alcun col vero
la dubia speme alquanto riconforta,
ch'el sia redito per altro sentiero
al loco ove s'invia la loro scorta.
Ne' petti ondeggia or questo or quel pensiero,
che fra paura e speme il cor traporta:
cosí raggio, che specchio mobil ferza,
per la gran sala or qua or là si scherza.

61

The youths who had remained in the forest, seeing heaven light up its stars, hearing the signal,
put an end to the hunt; each hastens to gather
in the traps and nets; then they group themselves in one path with their prey; they think only about exchanging boasts: lies are cheaply
bought and sold; then, all search among themselves for fair Julio.

62

Not seeing his dear companion, each freezes in
sudden fear lest some fierce beast or another
cruel accident should hinder his return. One
lights torches, one trumpets his horn, one calls
him loudly through the dark wood; the far-
striking voices multiply and the valleys answer:
"Julio, Julio."

63

Each stands uncertain in fear, frozen completely, except that he keeps calling; they see the sky
covered with shadows; despite their desire, they
do not know where to search. Still the great
wilderness resounds with "Julio, Julio"; the
wretched folk do not know what else to do. But,
after spending much of the night in vain, they
mournfully take the return path.

64

They go quietly, and some comfort their doubt-
ful hope with the truth that he has returned by
another path to their destination. Now this
thought and now that surges like a wave in
their breasts, their hearts waver between fear
and hope: as a ray of light striking a moving mirror plays now here, now there about a great hall.

LXV

Ma 'l gioven, che provato avea già l'arco
ch'ogni altra cura sgombra fuor del petto,
d'altre speme e paure e pensier carco,
era arrivato alla magion soletto.
Ivi pensando al suo novello incarco
stava in forti pensier tutto ristretto,
quando la compagnia piena di doglia
tutta pensosa entrò dentro alla soglia.

LXVI

Ivi ciascun piú da vergogna involto
per li alti gradi sen va lento lento:
quali i pastori a cui il fer lupo ha tolto
il piú bel toro del cornuto armento,
tornonsi a lor signor con basso volto,
né s'ardiscon d'entrar all'uscio drento;
stan sospirosi e di dolor confusi,
e ciascun pensa pur come sé scusi.

LXVII

Ma tosto ognuno allegro alzò le ciglia,
veggendo salvo lí sí caro pegno:
tal si fe', poi che la sua dolce figlia
ritrovò, Ceres giú nel morto regno.
Tutta festeggia la lieta famiglia
con essi, e Iulio di gioir fa segno,
e quanto el può nel cor preme sua pena
e il volto di letizia rasserena.

LXVIII

Ma fatta Amor la sua bella vendetta,
mossesi lieto pel negro aere a volo,
e ginne al regno di sua madre in fretta,
ov'è de' picciol suoi fratei lo stuolo:
al regno ov'ogni Grazia si diletta,
ove Biltà di fiori al crin fa brolo,
ove tutto lascivo, drieto a Flora,
Zefiro vola e la verde erba infiora.

But the youth, who had now felt the bow that
removes all other care from the breast, laden
with far other hopes and fears and thoughts, had
arrived all alone at his house. There, contemplat-
ing his new burden, he stood wrapped in heavy
thought, when his company, filled with distress
and concern, crossed the threshold.

66
There, overcome with shame, each slowly went
up the high steps: as shepherds, from whom the
fierce wolf has taken the most beautiful bull of
their horned herd, return to their lord with a
downcast face, nor dare to enter inside the door;
they stand sighing and confused with grief, and
each thinks how to excuse himself.

67
But soon each raised his brow in gladness, seeing
safe so dear a charge: so Ceres appeared, after
she had found her sweet daughter below in the
realm of Death. The glad household rejoices
with them and Julio seems to rejoice, pressing
down the pain inside his heart as best he can, he
makes his face serene with happiness.

68
But Love, having accomplished his fair vengeance, flew happily through the black air and
went in haste to the realm of his mother, the
home of his thronging little brothers: to the
realm where every Grace delights, where Beauty
weaves a garland of flowers about her hair,
where lascivious Zephyr flies behind Flora and
decks the green grass with flowers.

*67/ so Ceres . . . in the realm
of Death*: After Pluto had
stolen away her daughter Proserpina to make her his queen
in the underworld, Ceres, the
goddess of fertility, abandoned her functions and laid
the earth barren. When re-
united with her child, she
relented, restoring the fields.

LXIX

Or canta meco un po' del dolce regno,
Erato bella, che 'l nome hai d'amore;
tu sola, benché casta, puoi nel regno
secura entrar di Venere e d'Amore;
tu de' versi amorosi hai sola il regno,
teco sovente a cantar viensi Amore;
e, posta giú dagli omer la faretra,
tenta le corde di tua bella cetra.

LXX

Vagheggia Cipri un dilettoso monte,
che del gran Nilo e sette corni vede
e 'l primo rosseggiar dell'orizonte,
ove poggiar non lice al mortal piede.
Nel giogo un verde colle alza la fronte,
sotto esso aprico un lieto pratel siede,
u' scherzando tra' fior lascive aurette
fan dolcemente tremolar l'erbette.

LXXI

Corona un muro d'or l'estreme sponde
con valle ombrosa di schietti arbuscelli,
ove in su' rami fra novelle fronde
cantano i loro amor soavi augelli.
Sentesi un grato mormorio dell'onde,
che fan duo freschi e lucidi ruscelli,
versando dolce con amar liquore,
ove arma l'oro de' suoi strali Amore.

LXXII

Né mai le chiome del giardino eterno
tenera brina o fresca neve imbianca;
ivi non osa entrar ghiacciato verno,
non vento o l'erbe o li arbuscelli stanca;
ivi non volgon gli anni il lor quaderno,
ma lieta Primavera mai non manca,
ch'e suoi crin biondi e crespi all'aura spiega,
e mille fiori in ghirlandetta lega.

69
Now fair Erato, you that take your name from
love, sing awhile with me of the sweet kingdom;
you alone, although chaste, may safely enter the
realm of Venus and Love; you alone rule over
love poetry; often Love himself comes to sing
with you; having put down the quiver from his
shoulder, he tries the strings of your beautiful
lyre.

70
A delightful mountain lords over the isle of Cyprus, it faces the seven mouths of the Nile and
the first reddening of the horizon; there no mortal foot is allowed to tread. Between its shoulders
a green hill raises its forehead, a sunny and happy meadow lies below, where gentle breezes,
playing among the flowers, make the grass sweetly tremble.

71
On the outer edges, a golden wall encircles a
valley shady with slender bushes, in whose
branches gentle birds sing of their loves among
fresh leaves. A welcome murmuring of waves
is heard, made by two cool and clear-flowing
streams, pouring out their sweet and bitter liq-
uid, into which Love dips the golden points of
his arrows.

72
Cold snow or tender frost never whitens the
locks of the eternal garden; icy winter dares not
enter there, nor does a wind ever wear against its
bushes or grass; here the years do not turn over
their calendar, but joyful Spring is never absent:
she unfolds her blonde and curling hair to the
breeze and ties a thousand flowers in a garland.

69/ *Erato*: The muse of love
poetry.
70/ *Cyprus*: The traditional
home of Venus and one of
the main centers of her cult
in antiquity.

LXXIII

Lungo le rive e frati di Cupido,
che solo uson ferir la plebe ignota,
con alte voci e fanciullesco grido
aguzzon lor saette ad una cota.
Piacere e Insidia, posati in sul lido,
volgono il perno alla sanguigna rota,
e 'l fallace Sperar col van Disio
spargon nel sasso l'acqua del bel rio.

LXXIV

Dolce Paura e timido Diletto,
dolce Ire e dolce Pace insieme vanno;
le Lacrime si lavon tutto il petto
e 'l fiumicello amaro crescer fanno;
Pallore smorto e paventoso Affetto
con Magreza si duole e con Affanno;
vigil Sospetto ogni sentiero spia,
Letizia balla in mezo della via.

LXXV

Voluttà con Belleza si gavazza,
va fuggendo il Contento e siede Angoscia
el ceco Errore or qua or là svolazza,
percuotesi il Furor con man la coscia;
la Penitenzia misera stramazza,
che del passato error s'è accorta poscia,
nel sangue Crudeltà lieta si ficca,
e la Desperazion se stessa impicca.

LXXVI

Tacito Inganno e simulato Riso
con Cenni astuti messaggier de' cori,
e fissi Sguardi, con pietoso viso,
tendon lacciuoli a Gioventú tra' fiori.
Stassi, col volto in sulla palma assiso,
el Pianto in compagnia de' suo' Dolori;
e quinci e quindi vola sanza modo
Licenzia non ristretta in alcun nodo.

Along the banks, Cupid's brothers, who only
wound the obscure common people, sharpen
their arrows on a whetstone with loud voices
and childish cries. Seated on the bank, Charm
and Intrigues turn the axle of the bloody wheel,
and false Hope with vain Desire spill the water
of the lovely stream upon the stone.

74

Sweet Fear and timid Delight, sweet Angers and
sweet Peace walk together; Tears wash their own
breasts with tears, making the bitter rivulet swell;
wan Pallor and fearful Affection mourn with
Leanness and Trouble; vigilant Suspicion spies
every path, Gaiety dances in the middle of the
road.

75

Pleasure revels with Beauty; Contentment flies
away and Anguish reigns; blind Error flutters
back and forth, Frenzy beats his thigh with his
hand; wretched Penitence, who too late has real-
ized her past error, falls down prostrate, Cruelty
happily immerses herself in blood; and Despair
hangs herself.

76

Silent Deception, simulated Laughter, Signals,
the astute messengers of hearts, and fixed Gazes,
with their piteous countenance, spread a trap
among the flowers for Youth. Weeping, accom-
panied by his Griefs, sits with his face in his
palm; and License, unrestrained by any ties, flies
about without direction.

LXXVII
Cotal milizia e tuoi figli accompagna
Venere bella, madre delli Amori.
Zefiro il prato di rugiada bagna,
spargendolo di mille vaghi odori:
ovunque vola, veste la campagna
di rose, gigli, violette e fiori;
l'erba di sue belleze ha maraviglia:
bianca, cilestra, pallida e vermiglia.

LXXVIII
Trema la mammoletta verginella
con occhi bassi, onesta e vergognosa;
ma vie piú lieta, piú ridente e bella,
ardisce aprire il seno al sol la rosa:
questa di verde gemma s'incappella,
quella si mostra allo sportel vezosa,
l'altra, che 'n dolce foco ardea pur ora,
languida cade e 'l bel pratello infiora.

LXXIX
L'alba nutrica d'amoroso nembo
gialle, sanguigne e candide viole;
descritto ha 'l suo dolor Iacinto in grembo,
Narcisso al rio si specchia come suole;
in bianca vesta con purpureo lembo
si gira Clizia palidetta al sole;
Adon rinfresca a Venere il suo pianto,
tre lingue mostra Croco, e ride Acanto.

LXXX
Mai rivestí di tante gemme l'erba
la novella stagion che 'l mondo aviva.
Sovresso il verde colle alza superba
l'ombrosa chioma u' el sol mai non arriva;
e sotto vel di spessi rami serba
fresca e gelata una fontana viva,
con sí pura, tranquilla e chiara vena,
che gli occhi non offesi al fondo mena.

This army accompanies your sons, fair Venus, mother of the cupids. Zephyr bathes the meadow with dew, spreading a thousand lovely fragrances: wherever he flies he clothes the countryside in roses, lilies, violets, and other flowers; the grass marvels at its own beauties, white, blue, pale, and red.

78

Chaste and modest, the virgin violet trembles with downcast eyes; but the rose, many times happier, laughing and lovely, dares to open her breast to the sun: this one wears a jeweled hat of green, that one, flirting, peeps out the window, another, that even now burned with sweet fire, falls languid and flowers the beautiful meadow.

79

With an amorous mist the dawn nourishes white, crimson, and yellow violets; Hyacinth has written his sorrow upon his breast; as usual, Narcissus mirrors himself in the stream; in a white gown hemmed with purple, pallid Clytia turns with the sun; Adonis renews his weeping to Venus, Crocus shows three tongues, and Acanthus laughs.

80

The new season which brings life to earth never reclothed the grass with all these gems. Above, the green hill proudly raises its shady treeses, where the sun never enters; beneath a veil of thick branches is a living fountain, icy and cold, that runs so pure, tranquil, and clear that the eye unimpeded may reach its bottom.

79/ The following flowers are the products of metamorphosis. *Hyacinth*: A beautiful Spartan youth, loved by Apollo, was accidently killed by the god while they played together at quoits. The flower's markings represent the letters AI AI, the words of the god's lamentation. *Narcissus*: Punished by Nemesis for spurning the love of Echo, Narcissus, when lying beside a clear mountain pool, fell in love with his own reflection and died from unrequited self-love. *Clytia*: A daughter of Oceanus, pined away for love of Apollo and was turned into a sunflower. *Adonis*: A handsome young hunter, beloved of Venus, was killed by a wild boar and became the anemone. *Crocus*: Died for the love of the nymph Smilax; *three tongues*: refers to the physical appearance of the flower. *Acanthus*: A nymph changed into a flower by Apollo for having refused his love.

LXXXI

L'acqua da viva pomice zampilla,
che con suo arco il bel monte sospende;
e, per fiorito solco indi tranquilla
pingendo ogni sua orma, al fonte scende:
dalle cui labra un grato umor distilla,
che 'l premio di lor ombre alli arbor rende;
ciascun si pasce a mensa non avara,
e par che l'un dell'altro cresca a gara.

LXXXII

Cresce l'abeto schietto e sanza nocchi
da spander l'ale a Borea in mezo l'onde;
l'elce che par di mèl tutta trabocchi,
e 'l laur che tanto fa bramar suo fronde;
bagna Cipresso ancor pel cervio gli occhi
con chiome or aspre, e già distese e bionde;
ma l'alber, che già tanto ad Ercol, piacque,
col platan si trastulla intorno all'acque.

LXXXIII

Surge robusto el cerro, et alto el faggio,
nodoso el cornio, e 'l salcio umido e lento;
l'olmo fronzuto, e 'l frassin pur selvaggio;
el pino alletta con suoi fischi il vento.
L'avorniol tesse ghirlandette al maggio,
ma l'acer d'un color non è contento;
la lenta palma serba pregio a' forti,
l'ellera va carpon co' piè distorti.

LXXXIV

Mostronsi adorne le vite novelle
d'abiti varie e con diversa faccia:
questa gonfiando fa crepar la pelle,
questa racquista le già perse braccia;
quella tessendo vaghe e liete ombrelle,
pur con pampinee fronde Apollo scaccia;
quella ancor monca piange a capo chino,
spargendo or acqua per versar poi vino.

81
The water gushes from an arch of living pumice
which supports the lovely mountain; and, paint-
ing its every track, it calmly descends in a flowery wake to the fountain: from whose lips is dis-
tilled a welcome humor that rewards the trees
for their shade; each feeds from a not ungener-
ous table, and one seems to grow in competition
with the other.

82
Smooth and without knots grows the fir, fit to
spread out winglike sails to Boreas in the middle
of the sea; the holm-oak which appears to over-
flow with honey, and the laurel which causes
its leaves to be so greatly desired; the Cypress,
with locks now harsh, once long and blonde,
still weeps for Apollo's stag; but the tree that
once so pleased Hercules takes delight with the
plane tree beside the water.

83
The turkey-oak rises robust, lofty the beech
knotty the cornel berry, wet and pliant the wil-
low; leafy the elm, and ever wild the ash; the
pine entices the wind with its whistling. The
flowering ash weaves garlands to May, but the
maple is not content with one color; the bending palm serves as a reward for the brave, the
ivy crawls on malformed feet.

84
The new vines show themselves adorned with
various clothing and in different aspects: this
one, swelling, cracks its skin, this one reacquires
lost arms; that one, weaving a lovely and happy
awning, drives out Apollo with grape leaves; one
that is yet maimed weeps with a bowed head,
shedding water now in order later to pour forth
wine.

82/ *Boreas*: the north wind.
the Cypress: Cyparissus killed
a stag sacred to the Carthaean
nymphs; Apollo changed the
grief-stricken youth into the
cypress, the tree of mourning. *the tree that once so
pleased Hercules*: The poplar, sacred to Hercules.

LXXXV
El chiuso e crespo bosso al vento ondeggia,
e fa la piaggia di verdura adorna;
el mirto, che sua dea sempre vagheggia,
di bianchi fiori e verdi capelli orna.
Ivi ogni fera per amor vaneggia,
l'un ver l'altro i montoni armon le corna:
l'un l'altro cozza, l'un l'altro martella,
davanti all'amorosa pecorella.

LXXXVI
E mughianti giovenchi a piè del colle
fan vie piú cruda e dispietata guerra,
col collo e il petto insanguinato e molle,
spargendo al ciel co' piè l'erbosa terra.
Pien di sanguigna schiuma el cinghial bolle
le larghe zanne arruota e il grifo serra,
e rugghia e raspa e, per piú armar sue forze,
frega il calloso cuoio a dure scorze.

LXXXVII
Pruovon lor punga e daini paurosi,
e per l'amata druda arditi fansi;
ma con pelle vergata, aspri e rabbiosi,
e tigri infuriati a ferir vansi;
sbatton le code e con occhi focosi
ruggendo i fier leon di petto dansi;
zufola e soffia il serpe per la biscia,
mentre ella con tre lingue al sol si liscia.

LXXXVIII
El cervio appresso alla Massilia fera
co' piè levati la sua sposa abbraccia;
fra l'erbe ove piú ride primavera,
l'un coniglio coll'altro s'accovaccia;
le semplicette lepri vanno a schiera,
de' can secure, ad amorosa traccia:
sí l'odio antico e 'l natural timore
ne' petti ammorza, quando vuole, Amore.

85
The dense and curling box-tree waves in the
wind, and adorns the shore with greenery; the
myrtle that forever yearns for its goddess adorns
its green tresses with white flowers. Here every
creature raves with love, the rams arm themselves with horns one against the other: one
butts another, one hammers another, in the presence of the amorous ewe.

86
At the foot of the hill, bellowing young bulls
wage a much more brutal and pitiless war, with
breast and neck wet and bloody, their hooves
scattering the grassy earth to the sky. The boar
boils with bloody foam, grinds his huge tusks,
and shuts his snout; he roars and rasps, and, to
arm himself further, he chafes his calloused hide
against rough bark.

87
The timid deer do battle and become bold for
their beloved paramour; with striped hides,
the fierce, raging tigers furiously rush to wound
each other; proud, roaring lions lash their tails
and fight face to face with fiery eyes; the serpent hisses and pants for his mate, while she
licks herself in the sun with her triple tongues.

88
Beside the Libyan lion, the stag raises its hooves
to embrace his mate; in the meadows where
spring smiles most, one rabbit nestles with another; safe from hounds, the simple hares go in
groups on their amorous chase; so does Love,
when he desires, abate ancient hatred and natural fear inside their breasts.

LXXXIX

E muti pesci in frotta van notando
dentro al vivente e tenero cristallo,
e spesso intorno al fonte roteando
guidon felice e dilettoso ballo;
tal volta sovra l'acqua, un po' guizzando,
mentre l'un l'altro segue, escono a gallo:
ogni loro atto sembra festa e gioco,
né spengon le fredde acque il dolce foco.

XC

Li augelletti dipinti intra le foglie
fanno l'aere addolcir con nuove rime,
e fra piú voci un'armonia s'accoglie
di sí beate note e sí sublime,
che mente involta in queste umane spoglie
non potria sormontare alle sue cime;
e dove Amor gli scorge pel boschetto,
salton di ramo in ramo a lor diletto.

XCI

Al canto della selva Ecco rimbomba,
ma sotto l'ombra che ogni ramo annoda,
la passeretta gracchia e a torno romba;
spiega il pavon la sua gemmata coda,
bacia el suo dolce sposo la colomba,
e bianchi cigni fan sonar la proda;
e presso alla sua vaga tortorella
il pappagallo squittisce e favella.

XCII

Quivi Cupido e' suoi pennuti frati,
lassi già di ferir uomini e dei,
prendon diporto, e colli strali aurati
fan sentire alle fere i crudi omei;
la dea Ciprigna fra' suoi dolci nati
spesso sen viene, e Pasitea con lei,
quetando in lieve sonno gli occhi belli
fra l'erbe e' fiori e' gioveni arbuscelli.

89
Schools of silent fish swim within the gentle
flowing crystal, and circling about the fountain,
they often lead a happy and delightful dance;
sometimes, as one follows another, lightly dart-
ing, they rise to the surface: their every action
seems a festive game, the cold waters do not ex-
tinguish love's sweet flame.

90
The bright-colored little birds among the leaves
sweeten the air with new rhymes, and from
many voices a harmony gathers, such blessed
and exalted music that minds wrapped in these
human vestments could not rise to its sublimity;
and wherever Love guides them in the wood,
they flutter at their pleasure from branch to
branch.

91
Echo resounds with the song of the forest, while
beneath a shade interwoven by all the branches,
the sparrow chatters and clamors about; the pea-
cock spreads his jeweled tail, the dove kisses her
sweet husband, the white swans make the shore
resound; and the parrot squeaks and chatters beside his pretty turtledove.

92
There Cupid and his winged brothers, weary
now of wounding men and gods, take sport,
and with their golden arrows draw forth from
the beasts cruel cries of woe; the Cyprian goddess often draws near her sweet sons with Pasithea beside her, the two of them soothe their
lovely eyes in light sleep among the grass, flowers, and young bushes.

92/ *Pasithea*: One of the three
Graces.

XCIII

Muove del colle, mansueta e dolce,
la schiena del bel monte, e sovra i crini
d'oro e di gemme un gran palazo folce,
sudato già nei cicilian camini.
Le tre Ore, che 'n cima son bobolce,
pascon d'ambrosia i fior sacri e divini:
né prima dal suo gambo un se ne coglie,
ch'un altro al ciel piú lieto apre le foglie.

XCIV

Raggia davanti all'uscio una gran pianta,
che fronde ha di smeraldo e pomi d'oro:
e pomi ch'arrestar fenno Atalanta,.
ch'ad Ippomene dienno il verde alloro.
Sempre sovresso Filomela canta,
sempre sottesso è delle Ninfe un coro;
spesso Imeneo col suon di sua zampogna
tempra lor danze, e pur le noze agogna.

XCV

La regia casa il sereno aier fende,
fiammeggiante di gemme e di fino oro,
che chiaro giorno a meza notte accende;
ma vinta è la materia dal lavoro.
Sovra a colonne adamantine pende
un palco di smeraldo, in cui già fuoro
aneli e stanchi, drento a Mongibello,
Sterope e Bronte et ogni lor martello.

XCVI

Le mura a torno d'artificio miro
forma un soave e lucido berillo;
passa pel dolce oriental zaffiro
nell'ampio albergo el dí puro e tranquillo;
ma il tetto d'oro, in cui l'estremo giro
si chiude, contro a Febo apre il vessillo;
per varie pietre il pavimento ameno
di mirabil pittura adorna il seno.

The spine of the beautiful mountain rises sweetly and gently from the hill, and atop its leafy
hair supports a great palace of gold and gems,
once sweated over in the furnaces of Sicily.
The three Hours, who are the gardeners of the
peak, sprinkle the divine and sacred flowers with
ambrosia: the moment one is gathered from its
stem, another, happier, opens its petals to heaven.

94

A tall tree shines before the gate, its branches
of emerald and its apples of gold: the apples
which made Atalanta stop, that gave Hippomenes the green laurel of victory. Above it Philomela
always sings, beneath it is always a chorus of
nymphs; often Hymen, seeking out marriages,
leads their dances to the sound of his reed pipe.

95

The royal house cleaves the cloudless air, flaming with jewels and fine gold that kindle bright
day at midnight; but the material is surpassed by
the workmanship. On adamantine pillars is suspended a platform of emeralds, which once
made Sterops and Brontes, with all their hammers, tired and breathless in Mongibello.

96

By marvelous artifice a lovely lucid beryl forms
the surrounding walls; pure and tranquil daylight
passes through sweet oriental sapphire into the
spacious house; the roof of gold which closes in
the uppermost floor forms a canopy against the
sun; the pleasing pavement adorns its breast with
various stones in wonderful design.

93/ *the furnaces of Sicily*: The
forge of Vulcan was located
underneath Mt. Etna.
94/ *Atalanta*: The daughter
of King Schoeneus of Boetia,
renowned for her swiftness
afoot; she consented to marry
only the man who could de-
feat her in a race. As she out-
distanced him, Hippomenes
threw in her path three golden
apples given him by Venus.
Atalanta stopped to pick
them up and Hippomenes
passed her, winning the race
and her hand. *Philomela*:
Raped by her brother-in-law
Tereus, Philomela was turned
into a nightingale. *Hymen*:
god of marriage.
95/ *Sterops and Brontes . . .
Mongibello*: The cyclopes
Sterops and Brontes were employed as Vulcan's workmen
inside Etna (Mongibello).

XCVII

Mille e mille color formon le porte,
di gemme e di sí vivi intagli chiare,
che tutte altre opre sarian roze e morte
da far di sé natura vergognare:
nell'una è insculta la 'nfelice sorte
del vecchio Celio; e in vista irato pare
suo figlio, e colla falce adunca sembra
tagliar del padre le feconde membra.

XCVIII

Ivi la Terra con distesi ammanti
par ch'ogni goccia di quel sangue accoglia,
onde nate le Furie e' fier Giganti
di sparger sangue in vista mostron voglia;
d'un seme stesso in diversi sembianti
paion le Ninfe uscite sanza spoglia,
pur come snelle cacciatrice in selva,
gir saettando or una or altra belva.

XCIX

Nel tempestoso Egeo in grembo a Teti
si vede il frusto genitale accolto,
sotto diverso volger di pianeti
errar per l'onde in bianca schiuma avolto;
e drento nata in atti vaghi e lieti
una donzella non con uman volto,
da zefiri lascivi spinta a proda,
gir sovra un nicchio, e par che 'l cel ne goda.

C

Vera la schiuma e vero il mar diresti,
e vero il nicchio e ver soffiar di venti;
la dea negli occhi folgorar vedresti,
e 'l cel riderli a torno e gli elementi;
l'Ore premer l'arena in bianche vesti,
l'aura incresparle e crin distesi e lenti;
non una, non diversa esser lor faccia,
come par ch'a sorelle ben confaccia.

97
Thousands and thousands of colors form the
doors, splendid with gems and with such vivid
carvings that all other works would be crude and
lifeless in comparison, and nature itself is put to
shame: on one is sculpted the unhappy fate of
old Celius; his son appears, angry in countenance, and with a curved scythe seems to cut
away the fertile members of his father.

98
There the Earth with her outstretched mantles
seems to gather up every drop of that blood,
whence are born the Furies and fierce Giants,
who show desire in their faces for bloodshed;
from the same seed, in various shapes, the
Nymphs appear to emerge unclothed: slim hunt-
resses in the woods, they run, shooting arrows at
now one, now another beast.

99
In the stormy Aegean, the genital member is
seen to be received in the lap of Tethys, to drift
across the waves, wrapped in white foam, beneath the various turnings of the planets; and
within, born with lovely and happy gestures, a
young woman with nonhuman countenance, is
carried on a conch shell, wafted to shore by
playful zephyrs; and it seems that heaven rejoices in her birth.

100
You would call the foam real, the sea real, real
the conch shell and real the blowing wind; you
would see the lightning in the goddess's eyes,
the sky and the elements laughing about her; the
Hours treading the beach in white garments, the
breeze curling their loosened and flowing hair;
their faces not one, not different, as befits sisters.

97–103/ The first series of
bas-reliefs depict the birth of
Venus. Cronus castrated his
father Uranus (*Celius*). The
testicles fell into the sea, pro-
ducing a foam from which
Venus emerged.
99/ *Tethys*: Goddess of the
sea, wife of the god Oceanus.

CI

Giurar potresti che dell'onde uscissi
la dea premendo colla destra il crino,
coll'altra il dolce pome ricoprissi;
e, stampata dal piè sacro e divino,
d'erbe e di fior l'arena si vestissi;
poi, con sembiante lieto e peregrino,
dalle tre ninfe in grembo fussi accolta,
e di stellato vestimento involta.

CII

Questa con ambe man le tien sospesa
sopra l'umide trezze una ghirlanda
d'oro e di gemme orientali accesa,
questa una perla alli orecchi accomanda;
l'altra al bel petto e' bianchi omeri intesa,
par che ricchi monili intorno spanda,
de' quai solien cerchiar lor proprie gole,
quando nel ciel guidavon le carole.

CIII

Indi paion levate inver le spere
seder sovra una nuvola d'argento:
l'aier tremante ti parria vedere
nel duro sasso, e tutto il cel contento;
tutti li dei di sua biltà godere,
e del felice letto aver talento:
ciascun sembrar nel volto meraviglia,
con fronte crespa e rilevate ciglia.

CIV

Nello estremo, se stesso el divin fabro
formò felice di sí dolce palma,
ancor dalla fucina irsuto e scabro,
quasi obliando per lei ogni salma,
con desire aggiugnendo labro a labro
come tutta d'amore gli ardessi l'alma:
e par vie maggior fuoco acceso in ello,
che quel ch'avea lasciato in Mongibello.

101

You could swear that the goddess had emerged
from the waves, pressing her hair with her right
hand, covering with the other her sweet mound
of flesh; and where the strand was imprinted by
her sacred and divine step, it had clothed itself
in flowers and grass; then with happy, more than
mortal features, she was received in the bosom
of the three nymphs and cloaked in a starry garment.

102

With both hands one nymph holds above the
spray-wet tresses a garland, burning with gold
and oriental gems, another adjusts pearls in her
ears; the third, intent upon those beautiful
breasts and white shoulders, appears to strew
round them the rich necklaces with which they
three girded their own necks when they used to
dance in a ring in heaven.

103

Thence they seem to be raised toward the heavenly spheres, seated upon a silver cloud: in the
hard stone you would seem to see the air trembling and all of heaven contented; every god
takes pleasure in her beauty and desires her happy bed: each face seems to marvel, with raised
eyebrows and wrinkled forehead.

104

Finally the divine artisan formed his self-portrait,
happy with such a sweet prize, still bristly and
scabrous from his furnace, as if forgetting every
labor for her, joining his lips with desire to hers,
as if his soul burned completely with love: and
there seems to be a much greater fire kindled
within him than the one that he had left in
Mongibello.

CV

Nell'altra in un formoso e bianco tauro
si vede Giove per amor converso
portarne il dolce suo ricco tesauro,
e lei volgere il viso al lito perso
in atto paventosa; e i bei crin d'auro
scherzon nel petto per lo vento avverso;
la vesta ondeggia, e indrieto fa ritorno,
l'una man tiene al dorso, e l'altra al corno.

CVI

Le 'gnude piante a sé ristrette accoglie
quasi temendo il mar che lei non bagne:
tale atteggiata di paura e doglie
par chiami invan le dolci sue compagne;
le qual rimase tra fioretti e foglie
dolenti Europa ciascheduna piagne.
«Europa», suona il lito, «Europa, riedi»,
e 'l tor nuota e talor li bacia e piedi.

CVII

Or si fa Giove un cigno or pioggia d'oro,
or di serpente o d'un pastor fa fede,
per fornir l'amoroso suo lavoro;
or transformarsi in aquila si vede,
come Amor vuole, e nel celeste coro
portar sospeso il suo bel Ganimede,
qual di cipresso ha il biondo capo avinto,
ignudo tutto e sol d'ellera cinto.

CVIII

Fassi Nettunno un lanoso montone,
fassi un torvo giovenco per amore;
fassi un cavallo il padre di Chirone,
diventa Febo in Tessaglia un pastore:
e 'n picciola capanna si ripone
colui ch'a tutto il mondo dà splendore,
né li giova a sanar sue piaghe acerbe
perch'e' conosca la virtú dell'erbe.

105

On the other side of the door, Jove, transformed
for love into a handsome white bull, is seen car-
rying off his sweet rich treasure, and she turns
her face toward the lost shore with a terrified
gesture; in the contrary wind her lovely golden
hair plays over her breasts; her garment waves in
the wind and blows behind her, one hand grasps
his back, the other his horn.

106

She gathers in her bare feet as if fearing lest the
sea wash over her: in such a pose of fear and
grief, she seems to call in vain to her dear companions; they, left behind among flowers and
leaves, each mournfully cry for Europa. "Europa," the shore resounds, "Europa, come back,"
the bull swims on, and now and then kisses her
feet.

107

Now Jove becomes a swan and now a shower of
gold, now he pretends to be a serpent or a shepherd to accomplish his amorous work; now, as
Love wills, he is seen to transform himself into
an eagle and to carry off into the celestial choir
the fair dangling Ganymede, whose blonde head
is bound with cypress, otherwise naked, girded
only with ivy.

107/ *Now Jove . . . amorous work*: The allusions are to Jupiter's love affairs with Leda, Danae, Proserpina, and Mnemosine.

108/ *Neptune*: Became a ram to seduce Theophane; he took the form of a bull to pursue the "Aeolia virgine" (*Metamorphoses* VI, 116) an epithet applied variously by commentators to both Canace and Arne. *the father of Chiron*: Saturn lay as a horse with the nymph Philyra, and from their union the centaur Chiron was born.

108

For love, Neptune turns himself into a woolly
ram, then into a sullen young bull; the father of
Chiron turns into a horse, Phoebus becomes a
shepherd in Thessaly: he who gives light to all
the world lives in the obscurity of a small hut,
nor does his knowledge of the virtues of herbs
help him cure his own bitter wounds.

CIX

Poi segue Dafne, e 'n sembianza si lagna
come dicessi: "O ninfa, non ten gire,
ferma il piè, ninfa, sovra la campagna,
ch'io non ti seguo per farti morire;
cosí cerva lion, cosí lupo agna,
ciascuna il suo nemico suol fuggire:
me perché fuggi, o donna del mio core,
cui di seguirti è sol cagione amore?"

CX

Dall'altra parte la bella Arianna
colle sorde acque di Teseo si duole,
e dell'aura e del sonno che la 'nganna;
di paura tremando, come suole
per picciol ventolin palustre canna,
pare in atto aver prese tai parole:
"Ogni fera di te meno è crudele,
ognun di te piú mi saria fedele".

CXI

Vien sovra un carro, d'ellera e di pampino
coverto Bacco, il qual duo tigri guidono,
e con lui par che l'alta arena stampino
Satiri e Bacche, e con voci alte gridono:
quel si vede ondeggiar, quei par che 'nciampino,
quel con un cembol bee, quelli altri ridono;
qual fa d'un corno e qual delle man ciotola,
quale ha preso una ninfa e qual si ruotola.

CXII

Sovra l'asin Silen, di ber sempre avido,
con vene grosse nere e di mosto umide,
marcido sembra sonnacchioso e gravido,
le luci ha di vin rosse infiate e fumide;
l'ardite ninfe l'asinel suo pavido
pungon col tirso, e lui con le man tumide
a' crin s'appiglia; e mentre sí l'aizono,
casca nel collo, e' satiri lo rizono.

Then he chases Daphne, his face complaining, as
if he were saying: "O nymph, do not run away,
hold your step in the field, nymph, I do not pursue to give you death; the deer from the lion,
the lamb from the wolf, each is thus accustomed
to flee its enemy: but why do you flee, o lady of
my heart, when love is the only reason for my
pursuit?"

110
On the other side, beautiful Ariadne complains
to the deaf waters of Theseus and of the breeze
and sleep which deceived her; trembling with
fear, like swamp cane in a slight wind, she seems
by her gesture to have spoken these words:
"Any beast is less cruel than you, anyone would
be more faithful to me."

111
Bacchus, covered with ivy and vine leaves, approaches on a chariot drawn by two tigers, and
beside him satyrs and bacchantes seem to im-
print the deep sand and shout with loud voices:
this one seems to waver, those to stumble, there
one drinks from a cymbal, those others laugh;
one uses a horn, another his own hands, as a
drinking bowl; one has captured a nymph, another wallows.

112
On his donkey, Silenus, always eager to drink,
seems drunk, sleepy, and heavy, his large veins
black and wet with new vintage, his eyes puffed
out red and smoky with wine; and the bold
nymphs spur his frightened little donkey with
wands, with his swollen hands he clings to its
mane; while they push on, he falls on its neck,
and the satyrs straighten him up.

110/ *Ariadne*: After she had
helped him to escape from
the labyrinth of the Minotaur
on Crete, Theseus abandoned
Ariadne on Naxos, where
Bacchus found and married
her.
112/ *Silenus*: A comic deity,
bald and pot-bellied, always
drunk, the teacher and constant companion of Bacchus.

CXIII

Quasi in un tratto vista amata e tolta
dal fero Pluto, Proserpina pare
sovra un gran carro, e la sua chioma sciolta
a' zefiri amorosi ventilare;
la bianca vesta in un bel grembo accolta
sembra i colti fioretti giú versare:
lei si percuote il petto, e 'n vista piagne,
or la madre chiamando or le compagne.

CXIV

Posa giú del leone il fero spoglio
Ercole, e veste di femminea gonna
colui che 'l mondo da greve cordoglio
avea scampato, et or serve una donna;
e può soffrir d'Amor l'indegno orgoglio
chi colli omer già fece al ciel colonna;
e quella man con che era a tenere uso
la clava ponderosa, or torce un fuso.

CXV

Gli omer setosi a Polifemo ingombrano
l'orribil chiome e nel gran petto cascono,
e fresche ghiande l'aspre tempie adombrano:
d'intorno a lui le sue pecore pascono,
né a costui dal cor già mai disgombrano
le dolce acerbe cur che d'amor nascono,
anzi, tutto di pianto e dolor macero,
siede in un freddo sasso a piè d'un acero.

CXVI

Dall'uno all'altro orecchio un arco face
il ciglio irsuto lungo ben sei spanne;
largo sotto la fronte il naso giace,
paion di schiuma biancheggiar le zanne;
tra' piedi ha 'l cane, e sotto il braccio tace
una zampogna ben di cento canne:
lui guata il mar che ondeggia, e alpestre note
par canti, e muova le lanose gote,

113
Proserpina appears, almost in a moment, to be
seen, loved, and carried away by fierce Pluto in
his great chariot; her loosened hair is blown
about by the amorous breezes; her white garment gathered into a fair lap seems to pour
down the flowers she has picked: she beats her
breast and appears to weep, now calling her
mother, now her companions.

114
Hercules puts aside the wild lion hide and clothes
himself in a woman's skirt, he who has rescued
the world from grave perils is now a lady's serv-
ant; and he is willing to suffer the unworthy
pride of Love, he who once made his shoulders
the column of heaven; and that hand accustomed
to the ponderous club now turns a spindle.

115
The bristling locks of Polyphemus cover his
hairy shoulders and fall onto his huge chest,
fresh acorns wreathe his harsh temples: his sheep
feed about him, nor can the bittersweet cares
that are born of love be ever removed from his
heart, but rather, weakened by weeping and
grief, he sits on a cold stone at the foot of a
maple.

116
His hairy brow makes an arch six spans long
from ear to ear; beneath his brow lies a broad
nose, his fanglike teeth seem white with foam;
his dog rests between his feet, and under his arm
a shepherd's pipe of over a hundred reeds lies
silent: he regards the waving sea, he seems to
sing a mountain tune, as he moves his woolly
cheeks,

114/ *Hercules . . . woman's
skirt*: To fulfill the penance
imposed upon him by Jupiter,
Hercules served for three
years in feminine clothing as
a maidservant to Omphale,
queen of Lydia. Poliziano,
following Ovid (*Fasti* II, 303–
58), places an erotic interpretation on the myth.
115/ *Polyphemus*: The cyclops, whom Ulysses later
tricks and blinds, here sings
for the love of Galatea, the
sea nymph. For the source
of this and the following two
stanzas, see *Metamorphoses*
XIII, 744 ff.

CXVII

e dica ch'ella è bianca piú che il latte,
ma piú superba assai ch'una vitella,
e che molte ghirlande gli ha già fatte,
e serbali una cervia molto bella,
un orsacchin che già col can combatte;
e che per lei si macera e sfragella,
e che ha gran voglia di saper notare
per andare a trovarla insin nel mare.

CXVIII

Duo formosi delfini un carro tirono:
sovresso è Galatea che 'l fren corregge,
e quei notando parimente spirono;
ruotasi attorno piú lasciva gregge:
qual le salse onde sputa, e quai s'aggirono,
qual par che per amor giuochi e vanegge;
la bella ninfa colle suore fide
di sí rozo cantor vezzosa ride.

CXIX

Intorno al bel lavor serpeggia acanto,
di rose e mirti e lieti fior contesto;
con varii augei sí fatti, che il lor canto
pare udir nelli orecchi manifesto:
né d'altro si pregiò Vulcan mai tanto,
né 'l vero stesso ha piú del ver che questo;
e quanto l'arte intra sé non comprende,
la mente imaginando chiaro intende.

CXX

Questo è 'l loco che tanto a Vener piacque,
a Vener bella, alla madre d'Amore;
qui l'arcier frodolente prima nacque,
che spesso fa cangiar voglia e colore,
quel che soggioga il cel, la terra e l'acque,
che tende alli occhi reti, e prende il core,
dolce in sembianti, in atti acerbo e fello,
giovene nudo, faretrato augello.

saying that she is whiter than milk, but even
prouder than a heifer, that he has made her
many garlands, that he keeps for her a very beautiful doe and a bear-cub that already can fight
with dogs; that he mortifies and torments himself for her, and that he has a great desire to
know how to swim in order to go forth and find
her even in the sea.

118
Two shapely dophins pull a chariot: on it sits
Galatea and wields the reins; as they swim, they
breath in unison; a more wanton flock circles
around them: one spews forth salt waves, others
swim in circles, one seems to cavort and play for
love; with her faithful sisters, the fair nymph
charmingly laughs at such a crude singer.

119
Acanthus interlaced with roses, myrtle, and gay
flowers, entwines about the lovely work; with
various birds so sculpted that one seems to hear
their song plainly in one's ears: Vulcan never es-
teemed any other of his works so highly, truth itself has not more truth than this; whatever the
art in itself does not contain, the mind, imagin-
ing, clearly understands.

120
This is the place that pleased Venus so greatly,
beautiful Venus, the mother of Love; here was
born the fraudulent archer who often changes
lovers' will and hue, he who subjugates the sky,
the earth, and waters, who spreads nets for the
eyes and captures the heart, sweet in appearance, in action harsh and cruel, a naked youth, a
quivered bird.

CXXI

Or poi che ad ale tese ivi pervenne,
forte le scosse, e giú calossi a piombo,
tutto serrato nelle sacre penne,
come a suo nido fa lieto colombo:
l'aier ferzato assai stagion ritenne
della pennuta striscia il forte rombo:
ivi racquete le triunfante ale,
superbamente inver la madre sale.

CXXII

Trovolla assisa in letto fuor del lembo,
pur mo' di Marte sciolta dalle braccia,
il qual roverso li giacea nel grembo,
pascendo gli occhi pur della sua faccia:
di rose sovra a lor pioveva un nembo
per rinnovarli all'amorosa traccia;
ma Vener dava a lui con voglie pronte
mille baci negli occhi e nella fronte.

CXXIII

Sovra e d'intorno i piccioletti Amori
scherzavon nudi or qua or là volando:
e qual con ali di mille colori
giva le sparte rose ventilando,
qual la faretra empiea de' freschi fiori,
poi sovra il letto la venía versando,
qual la cadente nuvola rompea
fermo in su l'ale, e poi giú la scotea.

CXXIV

Come avea delle penne dato un crollo,
cosí l'erranti rose eron riprese:
nessun del vaneggiar era satollo;
quando apparve Cupido ad ale tese,
ansando tutto, e di sua madre al collo
gittossi, e pur co' vanni el cor li accese,
allegro in vista, e sí lasso ch'a pena
potea ben, per parlar, riprender lena.

121
Now, when he had arrived on outstretched wings,
he shook them strongly and plummeted down,
all enclosed in his sacred feathers, as a happy
dove swoops to its nest; for some time the beat-
en air retained the thunder of his feathered track:
there, quieting his triumphant wings, he went up
proudly toward his mother.

122
He found her seated on the edge of her couch,
just then released from the embrace of Mars,
who lay on his back in her lap, still feeding his
eyes on her face: a cloud of roses showered
down upon them to renew them for their amorous pursuits; but Venus with ready desires was
giving him a thousand kisses on his eyes and
forehead.

123
And little naked cupids played above and about,
flying here and there: and one with wings of a
thousand colors fanned about the scattered
roses, one filled his quiver with the fresh flowers, then poured it out over the bed, one stopped
the falling cloud upon his wings, and then pro-
ceeded to shake it down.

124
As he shook his feathers, the fall of roses was re-
sumed: no one was sated with the dalliance;
when, panting heavily, Cupid appeared with
wings extended, and threw himself on his mother's neck, and even with the beating of his wings
he inflamed her heart, happy in countenance,
and so weary he could hardly catch his breath
to speak.

CXXV

«Onde vien, figlio, o qual n'apporti nuove? —
Vener li disse, e lo baciò nel volto:
— Onde esto tuo sudor? qual fatte hai pruove?
qual dio, qual uomo hai ne' tuo' lacci involto?
Fai tu di nuovo in Tiro mughiar Giove?
o Saturno ringhiar per Pelio folto?
Che che ciò sia, non umil cosa parmi,
o figlio, o sola mia potenzia et armi.»

"Where do you come from, my son? What news
do you bring?" Venus asked him and kissed his
face: "Whence comes this sweat of yours? What
deeds have you done? What god, what man have
you caught in your snares? Do you make Jove
bellow again in Tyre? or Saturn neigh on thick-
eted Pelion? Whatever it is, it does not seem to
me an unimportant thing, my son, my only
power and arms."

BOOK TWO

I

Eron già tutti alla risposta intenti
e pargoletti intorno all'aureo letto,
quando Cupido con occhi ridenti,
tutto protervo nel lascivo aspetto,
si strinse a Marte, e colli strali ardenti
della faretra gli ripunse il petto,
e colle labra tinte di veleno
baciollo, e 'l fuoco suo gli misse in seno.

II

Poi rispose alla madre: «E' non è vana
la cagion che sí lieto a te mi guida:
ch'i' ho tolto dal coro di Diana
el primo conduttor, la prima guida,
colui di cui gioir vedi Toscana,
di cui già insino al ciel la fama grida,
insino agl'Indi, insino al vecchio Mauro:
Iulio, minor fratel del nostro Lauro.

III

L'antica gloria e 'l celebrato onore
chi non sa della Medica famiglia,
e del gran Cosmo, italico splendore,
di cui la patria sua si chiamò figlia?
E quanto Petro al paterno valore
n'aggiunse pregio, e con qual maraviglia
dal corpo di sua patria rimosse abbia
le scelerate man, la crudel rabbia?

IV

Di questo e della nobile Lucrezia
nacquene Iulio, e pria ne nacque Lauro:
Lauro che ancor della bella Lucrezia
arde, e lei dura ancor si mostra a Lauro,
rigida piú che a Roma già Lucrezia,
o in Tessaglia colei che è fatta un lauro;
né mai degnò mostrar di Lauro agli occhi
se non tutta superba e suo' begli occhi.

1

Now attentive to his response were all the little
putti about the golden couch, when Cupid, his
eyes laughing, his demeanor petulant and wanton, embraced Mars and again pierced his breast
with the burning arrows of his quiver, and kissed
him with lips tinged with venom, planting his
fire in the other's breast.

2

Then he answered his mother: "No fruitless
reason brings me so happy unto you: for I have
taken from the chorus of Diana its foremost
leader and guide, he in whom you see Tuscany
rejoice, whom Fame already shouts to the heavens unto the Indies, unto the aged Moor: Julio,
the younger brother of our Laurel.

3

"Who is not aware of the ancient glory and renowned honor of the Medici family, and of great
Cosimo, the splendor of Italy, whose city calls
herself his daughter? And how much esteem has
Piero added to his father's worth, with what mir-
aculous means has he removed evil hands and
cruel discord from the body of the state?

4

"From Piero and the noble Lucrezia, Julio was
born and, before him, Laurel: Laurel, who still
burns for a beautiful Lucrezia, while she still
shows herself hardhearted to Laurel, more unbending than the Lucretia once of Rome or than
she who became a laurel in Thessaly; nor has she
ever deigned, unless haughtily, to show her beautiful eyes to the eyes of Laurel.

2/ *unto the Indies, unto the aged Moor*: From east to west; the aged Moor is the titan Atlas, changed into the Moroccan mountain chain bearing his name.
3/ *Cosimo*: Cosimo de' Medici (1389–1464) established his banking family as the virtual rulers of Florence. *Piero*: Piero de' Medici (1416–1469), Cosimo's son and the father of Lorenzo and Giuliano. *evil hands*: Poliziano alludes to the 1466 conspiracy among several leading Florentine families, allied with Borso d'Este, Duke of Ferrara, to assassinate Piero and wrest control of the city from the Medici. The plot was discovered and averted by the seventeen-year-old Lorenzo, and the chief conspirators were sent into exile.
4/ *Lucrezia*: The noble Lucrezia is Lucrezia Tornabuoni (I, 3). The beautiful Lucrezia is Lucrezia Donati, Lorenzo's mistress and lady of his sonnets. The Roman Lucrezia (Lucretia) was the chaste matron who committed suicide after she was raped by Tarquin (Livy I, lviii). *laurel in Thessaly*: Daphne. The octave repeats its rhyme words: Lauro, Lucrezia, occhi.

V

Non priego non lamento al meschin vale,
ch'ella sta fissa come torre al vento,
perch'io lei punsi col piombato strale,
e col dorato lui, di che or mi pento;
ma tanto scoterò, madre, queste ale,
che 'l foco accenderolli al petto drento:
richiede ormai da noi qualche restauro
la lunga fedeltà del franco Lauro,

VI

che tutt'or parmi pur veder pel campo,
armato lui, armato el corridore,
come un fer drago gir menando vampo,
abatter questo e quello a gran furore,
l'armi lucenti sue sparger un lampo
che tremar faccin l'aier di splendore;
poi, fatto di virtute a tutti essemplo,
riportarne il trionfo al nostro templo.

VII

E che lamenti già le Muse ferno,
e quanto Apollo s'è già meco dolto
ch'i' tenga il lor poeta in tanto scherno!
et io con che pietà suo' versi ascolto!
ch'i' l'ho già visto al piú rigido verno,
pien di pruina e crin, le spalle e 'l volto,
dolersi colle stelle e colla luna,
di lei, di noi, di suo crudel fortuna.

VIII

Per tutto el mondo ha nostre laude sparte,
mai d'altro mai se non d'amor ragiona;
e potea dir le tue fatiche, o Marte,
le trombe e l'arme, e 'l furor di Bellona;
ma volle sol di noi vergar le carte,
e di quella gentil ch'a dir lo sprona:
ond'io lei farò pia, madre, al suo amante,
ch'i' pur son tuo, non nato d'adamante.

5

"Neither prayer nor lament avails the wretch,
for she stands fixed as a tower before the wind:
I pierced her with a leaden arrow while I wounded him with one of gold, deeds I now repent:
but I will so shake these wings, mother, that I
will kindle a fire inside her breast. The long-suf-
fering faith of noble Laurel merits some reward
from us,

6

"for I seem to see him in the field just now, he
and his steed are armed; like a fierce dragon
spewing flames, he beats down this man and that
one with great fury, his brilliant armour flashes
and makes the air tremble with light; then, having set an example of valor for all, he carries his
triumph to our temple.

7

"What laments the Muses made, how much has
Apollo grieved to me, that I should hold their
poet in such disdain! And with what pity I listen
to his verses! For in starkest winter I have seen
him, his hair, shoulders, and face full of frost,
complain to the stars and moon of her, of us, of
his cruel fortune.

8

"He has spread our praises throughout the world,
never, never does he speak of anything else but
love; while he could tell of your labors, Mars,
the trumpets, arms, and fury of Bellona; yet he
has wished to pen his paper only of us and of
that noble she who spurs him on to write:
wherefore, Mother, I shall make her take pity on
her lover, for I am your son, not born of hard
diamond.

5/ *I pierced her . . . one of gold*: According to Ovid (*Met.* I, 468–71) the first arrow "puts to flight, the other kindles love."
8/ *Bellona*: The goddess of war.

IX

I' non son nato di ruvida scorza,
ma di te, madre bella, e son tuo figlio;
né crudele essere deggio, e lui mi sforza
a riguardarlo con pietoso ciglio.
Assai provato ha l'amorosa forza,
assai giaciuto è sotto 'l nostro artiglio;
giust'è ch'e' faccia ormai co' sospir triegua,
e del suo buon servir premio consegua.

X

Ma 'l bel Iulio ch'a noi stato è ribello,
e sol di Delia ha seguito el trionfo,
or drieto all'orme del suo buon fratello
vien catenato innanzi al mio trionfo;
né mosterrò già mai pietate ad ello
finché ne porterà nuovo trionfo:
ch'i' gli ho nel cor diritta una saetta
dagli occhi della bella Simonetta.

XI

E sai quant'è nel petto e nelle braccia,
quanto sopra 'l destriero è poderoso:
pur mo' lo vidi sí feroce in caccia,
che parea il bosco di lui paventoso;
tutta aspreggiata avea la bella faccia,
tutto adirato, tutto era focoso.
Tal vid'io te là sovra el Termodonte
cavalcar, Marte, e non con esta fronte.

XII

Questa è, madre gentil, la mia vittoria;
quinci è 'l mio travagliar, quinci è 'l sudore;
cosí va sovra al cel la nostra gloria,
el nostro pregio, el nostro antico onore;
cosí mai scancellata la memoria
fia di te, madre, e del tuo figlio Amore;
cosí canteran sempre e versi e cetre
li stral, le fiamme, gli archi e le faretre.»

9

"I am not born of rough bark, but from you, my
beautiful mother, and I am your son; I should
not be cruel, and he constrains me to regard him
with a merciful eye. He has long experienced the
force of love, long has he lain beneath our talon;
now it is just that he make a truce with sighs and
attain the reward of good service.

10

"But handsome Julio, who has been a rebel unto
us, and followed only Delia's triumph, now, following his good brother's steps, comes chained
in the forefront of my triumph; I will not show
any pity to him until he carries off a new triumph for us: for I have shot an arrow into his
heart from the eyes of the fair Simonetta.

11

"And you know what his arms and shoulders
are, how powerful he is on horseback: even now
I saw him so ferocious in the hunt that the
woods seemed afraid of him; his comely face
had become all harsh, irate, and fiery. Such were
you, Mars, when I saw you riding along the
Thermodon, not as you are now.

12

"This, noble Mother, is my victory; this has been
my toil and my sweat; for which our glory, our
reputation, our ancient honor will rise above the
heavens; for which your memory, Mother, and
that of your son, Love, will never be erased; for
which verses and lyres will forever sing of our
arrows, flames, bows, and quivers."

10/ *Delia*: Diana.
11/ *Thermodon*: A river in
Cappadocia, sacred to Mars.

XIII

Fatta ella allor piú gaia nel sembiante,
balenò intorno uno splendor vermiglio,
da fare un sasso divenire amante,
non pur te, Marte; e tale ardea nel ciglio,
qual suol la bella Aurora fiammeggiante;
poi tutto al petto si ristringe el figlio,
e trattando con man suo chiome bionde,
tutto el vagheggia e lieta li risponde:

XIV

«Assai, bel figlio, el tuo desir m'agrada,
che nostra gloria ognor piú l'ale spanda;
chi erra torni alla verace strada,
obligo è di servir chi ben comanda.
Pur convien che di nuovo in campo vada
Lauro, e si cinga di nuova ghirlanda:
ché virtú nelli affanni piú s'accende,
come l'oro nel fuoco piú risplende.

XV

Ma prima fa mestier che Iulio s'armi
sí che di nostra fama el mondo adempi;
e tal del forte Achille or canta l'armi
e rinnuova in suo stil gli antichi tempi,
che diverrà testor de' nostri carmi,
cantando pur degli amorosi essempi:
onde la gloria nostra, o bel figliuolo,
vedrèn sopra le stelle alzarsi a volo.

XVI

E voi altri, mie' figli, al popol tosco
lieti volgete le trionfante ale,
giten tutti fendendo l'aer fosco;
tosto prendete ognun l'arco e lo strale,
di Marte el dolce ardor sen venga vosco.
Or vedrò, figli, qual di voi piú vale:
gite tutti a ferir nel toscan coro
ch'i' serbo a qual fie 'l primo un arco d'oro.»

13

She, then, with a happier face, blushed so that a
vermilion glow flashed about, such as to make a
stone in love, not only you, Mars; her eyes
burned like the lovely flaming dawn; then she
presses her son to her breast, fondling his golden
locks with her hand, she makes much of him,
and joyfully answers:

14

"Much, my fair son, does your desire please me,
that our glory should spread its wings ever farther; let the errant one return to the true path:
one is obliged to serve a just commander.
Still it befits Laurel to go into the field once
more and crown himself with a new wreath,
for virtue proves itself greater in trials, as gold
shines the more in fire.

15

"But first Julio should arm himself, so that he
may fill the world with our fame; and one is
now singing the arms of strong Achilles and with
his style is renewing ancient times, who will become the maker of our hymns, ever singing the
examples of love: whence we shall see our glory,
my fair son, rise in flight above the stars.

16

"And you, my other sons, happily turn your triumphant wings toward the Tuscan people, go,
break through the night air; each of you quickly
take a bow and arrow, let the sweet ardor of
Mars go with you. Now I shall see, my sons,
which among you is most worthy: go, all of you,
and wound the Tuscan ranks; I shall give a gold-
en bow to the foremost."

15/ *strong Achilles*: Another
reference to Poliziano's translation of the *Iliad*.

XVII
Tosto al suo dire ognuno arco e quadrella
riprende, e la faretra al fianco alluoga,
come, al fischiar del comito, sfrenella
la 'gnuda ciurma e remi, e mette in voga.
Già per l'aier ne va la schiera snella,
già sopra la città calon con foga:
così e vapor pel bel seren giú scendono,
che paion stelle mentre l'aier fendono.

XVIII
Vanno spiando gli animi gentili
che son dolce esca all'amoroso foco;
sovress'e' batton forte i lor fucili,
e fanli apprender tutti a poco a poco.
L'ardor di Marte ine' cor giovenili
s'affige, e quelli infiamma del suo gioco;
e mentre stanno involti nel sopore,
pare a' gioven far guerra per Amore.

XIX
E come quando il sol li Pesci accende,
tutta la terra è di suo virtú pregna,
che poscia a primavera fuor si estende,
mostrando al cel verde e fiorita insegna;
cosi ne' petti ove lor foco scende
s'abbarbica un disio che drento regna,
un disio sol d'eterna gloria e fama,
che le 'nfiammate menti a virtú chiama.

XX
Esce sbandita la Viltà d'ogni alma,
e, benché tarda sia, Pigrizia fugge;
a Libertate l'una e l'altra palma
legon gli Amori, e quella irata rugge.
Solo in disio di gloriosa palma
ogni cor giovenil s'accende e strugge;
e dentro al petto sorpriso dal sonno
li spirite' d'amor posar non ponno.

17
Promptly, at her command, each takes his bow
and arrows and places his quiver at his side, as,
at the whistling of the boatswain, the naked
crew unships oars and starts rowing. Now the
swift flock goes through the air; now they fall
upon the city in a rush: as vapors descend
through the fair calm air, that seem to be stars
as they pierce the sky.

18
They go, searching out noble minds, that are the
sweet tinder for the flames of love; they strike
their flints against them and little by little make
them catch fire. The ardor of Mars catches in
those young hearts and inflames them for his
games; while they are wrapped in sleep, it seems
to the youths that they are waging war for Love.

19
As in the season when the sun lights up the
Fishes, the entire earth teems with his vitality,
to later unfold in Spring, displaying to the sky
its green and flowery insignia; so in the breasts
where their fire descends, a desire takes root
which rules within, a desire only for eternal
glory and fame, which incites minds thus inflamed to virtue.

20
Banished, Baseness leaves every soul, and Sloth
flees, although lazy; the cupids tie the hands of
Liberty and she roars enraged. Desiring only the
glorious palm, every young breast burns and
languishes; within a heart captured in sleep, the
little spirits of love can find no rest.

17/ *vapors*: Shooting stars
were attributed to burning
vapors.

XXI

E cosí mentre ognun dormendo langue,
ne' lacci è 'nvolto onde già mai non esce;
ma come suol fra l'erba el picciol angue
tacito errare, o sotto l'onde el pesce,
sí van correndo per l'ossa e pel sangue
gli ardenti spiritelli, e 'l foco cresce.
Ma Vener, com'e suo' alati corrieri
vide partiti, mosse altri pensieri.

XXII

Pasitea fe' chiamar, del Sonno sposa,
Pasitea, delle Grazie una sorella,
Pasitea che dell'altre è piú amorosa,
quella che sovra a tutte è la piú bella;
e disse: «Muovi, o ninfa graziosa,
truova el consorte tuo, veloce e snella:
fa che e' mostri al bel Iulio tale imago,
che 'l facci di mostrarsi al campo vago.»

XXIII

Cosí le disse; e già la ninfa accorta
correa sospesa per l'aier serena;
quete sanza alcun rombo l'ale porta,
e lo ritruova in men che non balena.
Al carro della Notte el facea scorta,
e l'aria intorno avea di Sogni piena,
di varie forme e stranier portamenti,
e facea racquetar li fiumi e i venti.

XXIV

Come la ninfa a' suoi gravi occhi apparve,
col folgorar d'un riso gliele aperse:
ogni nube dal ciglio via disparve,
che la forza del raggio non sofferse.
Ciascun de' Sogni drento alle lor larve
gli si fe' incontro, e 'l viso discoverse;
ma lei, poi che Morfeo con gli altri scelse,
gli chiese al Sonno, e tosto indi si svelse.

21
And thus, while one languishes as he sleeps, he
is trapped by snares from which he will never escape; but as a little snake wanders silently
through the grass, or a fish under water, so the
ardent spirits run through blood and marrow,
and the fire grows. But Venus, as she saw her
winged messengers depart, pondered other
thoughts.

22
She called Pasithea, the wife of Sleep, Pasithea,
one of the sister Graces, Pasithea, more amorous
than the others, the most beautiful of all; and
said to her: "Go, o gracious nymph, swift and
nimble, find your husband: have him show Julio
such an image as will make him yearn to show
his valor on the field."

23
Thus she spoke; and already the clever nymph
ran suspended through the clear air; she carries
her wings quietly without a sound, and finds
him in less time than a flash of lightning. He was
escorting the chariot of Night and the surrounding air was filled with Dreams of various forms
and strange bearing, and he was quieting the riv-
ers and winds.

24
As the nymph appeared before his heavy eyes,
she opened them with the lightning of a smile:
unable to endure the force of that light, every
cloud disappeared from his eyelids. Each of the
Dreams inside its ghostlike form confronted her
and showed its face; but she, after choosing Mor-
pheus and some others, requested them of Sleep,
and quickly moved away.

XXV

Indi si svelse, e di quanto convenne
tosto ammonilli, e partí sanza posa;
a pena tanto el ciglio alto sostenne,
che fatta era già tutta sonnacchiosa;
vassen volando sanza muover penne,
e ritorna a sua dea, lieta e gioiosa.
Gli scelti Sogni ad ubidir s'affrettono,
e sotto nuove fogge si rassettono:

XXVI

quali i soldati che di fuor s'attendono,
quando sanza sospetto et arme giacciono,
per suon di tromba al guerreggiar s'accendono,
vestonsi le corazze e gli elmi allacciono,
e giú dal fianco le spade sospendono,
grappon le lance e' forti scudi imbracciono;
e cosí divisati i destrier pungono
tanto ch'alla nimica schiera giungono.

XXVII

Tempo era quando l'alba s'avicina,
e divien fosca l'aria ove era bruna;
e già 'l carro stellato Icaro inchina,
e par nel volto scolorir la luna:
quando ciò ch'al bel Iulio el cel destina
mostrono i Sogni, e sua dolce fortuna;
dolce all'entrar, all'uscir troppo amara,
però che sempre dolce al mondo è rara.

XXVIII

Pargli veder feroce la sua donna,
tutta nel volto rigida e proterva,
legar Cupido alla verde colonna
della felice pianta di Minerva,
armata sopra alla candida gonna,
che 'l casto petto col Gorgon conserva;
e par che tutte gli spennecchi l'ali,
e che rompa al meschin l'arco e li strali.

25
She moved away, quickly advised them what
was needed, and left without delay; she could
scarcely keep her own eyelids open, she was already steeped in sleep; she flies off without moving her wings, and returns, joyous and happy, to
her goddess. The chosen Dreams hurry to obey,
disposing themselves in new shapes:

26
just as soldiers camped in their tents outside a
city that lie about without cares or armour, at
the sound of a trumpet burn to fight, don their
breastplates and lace their helmets, hang their
swords at their sides, seize their lances and thrust
their arms into their strong shields; and, falling
into columns, they spur their horses until they
reach the enemy troops.

27
It was the time when dawn approaches, and the
air becomes gray where it has been brown; and
now Icarus bends down his starry chariot and
the moon appears to grow pale: when the
Dreams reveal what heaven destines for fair Julio
and his sweet fortune; sweet at the beginning, at
the end too bitter, for lasting sweetness in this
world is rare.

28
He seems to see his lady, harsh and unbending in
aspect, fiercely tie Cupid to the green trunk of
Minerva's happy tree; over her white gown she
wears armour which protects her chaste bosom
with its gorgon breastplate; and she seems to
pluck all the feathers from his wings, and she
breaks the bow and arrows of the wretch.

27/ *Icarus*: A star of the
northern constellation Bootes
(I, 5) which sets toward morning. The dawn was traditionally the time of true dreams.
28/ *Minerva's happy tree*:
The olive tree. *gorgon breastplate*: Simonetta is protected
by the armour of Minerva,
symbolizing reason and chastity. Minerva placed the head
of the gorgon Medusa, killed
by Perseus, upon her aegis.

XXIX

Ahimè, quanto era mutato da quello
Amor che mo' tornò tutto gioioso!
Non era sovra l'ale altero e snello,
non del trionfo suo punto orgoglioso:
anzi merzé chiamava el meschinello
miseramente, e con volto pietoso
gridando a Iulio: «Miserere mei,
difendimi, o bel Iulio, da costei.»

XXX

E Iulio a lui dentro al fallace sonno
parea risponder con mente confusa:
«Come poss'io ciò far, dolce mio donno,
ché nell'armi di Palla è tutta chiusa?
Vedi i mie' spirti che soffrir non ponno
la terribil sembianza di Medusa,
e 'l rabbioso fischiar delle ceraste,
e 'l volto e l'elmo e 'l folgorar dell'aste.»

XXXI

«Alza gli occhi, alza, Iulio, a quella fiamma
che come un sol col suo splendor t'adombra:
quivi è colei che l'alte mente infiamma,
e che de' petti ogni viltà disgombra.
Con essa, a guisa di semplice damma,
prenderai questa ch'or nel cor t'ingombra
tanta paura, e t'invilisce l'alma;
ché sol ti serba lei trionfal palma.»

XXXII

Cosí dicea Cupido, e già la Gloria
scendea giú folgorando ardente vampo:
con essa Poesia, con essa Istoria
volavon tutte accese del suo lampo.
Costei parea ch'ad acquistar vittoria
rapissi Iulio orribilmente in campo,
e che l'arme di Palla alla sua donna
spogliassi, e lei lasciassi in bianca gonna.

29
Alas, how changed he was from that Love who
just now had joyfully returned! He was not
haughtily and nimbly soaring, he was not at all
gloating over his triumph: rather the little wretch
was crying miserably for mercy, and called to
Julio with a woeful countenance: "Have pity on
me, defend me from her, fair Julio."

30
And Julio within his false dream seemed to answer him with a confused mind: "How may I do
this, my sweet lord, for she is all enclosed in the
armour of Pallas? You see my spirits cannot endure the terrible features of Medusa, the angry
hiss of her vipers, the face, the helmet, and the
flashing lance."

31
"Raise, raise your eyes, Julio, to that flame
which, like a sun, dazzles you with its bright-
ness: there is she who inflames lofty minds and
removes all baseness from the heart. With her
you will capture, as you would a simple doe, this
lady who now so burdens your heart with fear
and makes base your soul; only a triumphal
palm will win her for you."

32
So Cupid was saying, and Glory was already des-
cending, flashing about a fierce splendor: Poetry
and History flew with her, kindled by her lightning. With dreadful force, she seemed to carry
Julio off to the battlefield to gain victory, she
seemed to strip the armour of Pallas from his
lady and left her in her white gown.

XXXIII

Poi Iulio di suo spoglie armava tutto,
e tutto fiammeggiar lo facea d'auro;
quando era al fin del guerreggiar condutto,
al capo gl'intrecciava oliva e lauro.
Ivi tornar parea suo gioia in lutto:
vedeasi tolto il suo dolce tesauro,
vedea suo ninfa in trista nube avolta,
dagli occhi crudelmente esserli tolta.

XXXIV

L'aier tutta parea divenir bruna,
e tremar tutto dello abisso il fondo;
parea sanguigno el cel farsi e la luna,
e cader giú le stelle nel profondo.
Poi vede lieta in forma di Fortuna
surger suo ninfa e rabbellirsi il mondo,
e prender lei di sua vita governo,
e lui con seco far per fama eterno.

XXXV

Sotto cotali ambagi al giovinetto
fu mostro de' suo' fati il leggier corso:
troppo felice, se nel suo diletto
non mettea morte acerba il crudel morso.
Ma che puote a Fortuna esser disdetto,
ch'a nostre cose allenta e stringe il morso?
Né val perch'altri la lusinghi o morda,
ch'a suo modo ne guida e sta pur sorda.

XXXVI

Adunque il tanto lamentar che giova?
A che di pianto pur bagnar le gote?
Se pur convien che lei ne guidi e muova,
se mortal forza contro a lei non puote,
se con sue penne il nostro mondo cova,
e tempra e volge, come vuol, le rote?
Beato qual da lei suo' pensier solve,
e tutto drento alla virtú s'involve!

33

Then she armed Julio with her spoils, and made
him blaze with gold; when he had reached the
end of his battle, she entwined the olive and
laurel around his head. There his joy seemed to
turn into mourning: he saw his sweet treasure
taken from him, he saw his nymph, enveloped in
a sad cloud, cruelly taken from before his eyes.

34

The air seemed to turn dark and the depths of
the abyss to tremble; the heavens and the moon
seemed to turn bloody, and the stars seemed to
fall into the deep. Then he sees his nymph rise
again, happy in the form of Fortune and the
world grows beautiful again: he sees her govern
his life, and make them both eternal through
fame.

35

In these confused signs the youth was shown
the changing course of his fate: too happy, if
early death were not placing its cruel bit on his
delight. But what can be gainsaid to Fortune
who slackens and pulls the reins of our affairs?
The flattery and curses of others do not prevail,
for she remains deaf and rules us as she pleases.

36

Therefore what can so much lamentation avail?
Why do we still bathe our cheeks in tears? If
need be that she must govern and move us, if
mortal force can do nothing against her, if she
broods over our world with her wings, and turns
and tempers her wheel as she wishes. Blessed is
he who frees his thoughts from her and encloses
himself completely within his own virtue!

XXXVII

O felice colui che lei non cura
e che a' suoi gravi assalti non si arrende,
ma come scoglio che incontro al mar dura,
o torre che da Borea si difende,
suo' colpi aspetta con fronte sicura,
e sta sempre provisto a sua vicende!
Da sé sol pende, e 'n se stesso si fida,
né guidato è dal caso, anzi lui guida.

XXXVIII

Già carreggiando il carro Aurora lieta
di Pegaso stringea l'ardente briglia;
surgea del Gange el bel solar pianeta,
raggiando intorno coll'aurate ciglia;
già tutto parea d'oro il monte Oeta,
fuggita di Latona era la figlia;
surgevon rugiadosi in loro stelo
li fior chinati dal notturno gelo.

XXXIX

La rondinella sovra al nido allegra,
cantando salutava il nuovo giorno;
e già de' Sogni la compagnia negra
a sua spilonca avean fatto ritorno;
quando con mente insieme lieta et egra
si destò Giulio e girò gli occhi intorno:
gli occhi intorno girò tutto stupendo,
d'amore e d'un disio di gloria ardendo.

XL

Pargli vedersi tuttavia davanti
la Gloria armata in su l'ale veloce
chiamare a giostra e valorosi amanti,
e gridar "Iulio Iulio" ad alta voce.
Già sentir pargli le trombe sonanti,
già divien tutto nell'arme feroce:
cosí tutto focoso in piè risorge,
e verso il cel cota' parole porge:

37

Happy he who pays no heed to her nor gives in
to her heavy assaults, but like a rock that stands
against the sea, or a tower that resists the north
wind, awaits her blows with an unconcerned
brow, always prepared for her changes! He depends only on himself, he trusts himself alone:
not governed by chance, he governs chance.

38

Already driving her chariot, cheerful Dawn was
holding tight the ardent bridle of Pegasus; the
fair solar planet was rising from the Ganges,
shining about him from his golden brow; now
all Mount Oeta seemed all gold, the daughter of
Latona had fled; the flowers, bent by nocturnal
frost, were rising dewy upon their stems.

39

On her nest, the happy swallow greeted the new
day with song; already the black troop of dreams
had returned to its cave; when with a mind both
joyful and sad, Julio awoke and gazed about: he
gazed about in wonderment, burning with love
and a desire for glory.

40

He seems to see still before him armed Glory on
rapid wings, calling the valorous lovers to joust
and loudly crying, "Julio, Julio." Already he
seems to hear the sounding trumpets, already he
becomes fierce in arms: all afire, he rises to his
feet, and sends these words to heaven:

38/ *Mount Oeta*: A mountain
chain in Thessaly. *the daughter of Latona*: Diana, the
moon.

XLI

«O sacrosanta dea, figlia di Giove,
per cui il tempio di Ian s'apre e riserra,
la cui potente destra serba e muove
intero arbitrio di pace e di guerra;
vergine santa, che mirabil pruove
mostri del tuo gran nume in cielo e 'n terra,
che i valorosi cuori a virtú infiammi,
soccorrimi or, Tritonia, e virtú dammi.

XLII

S'io vidi drento alle tue armi chiusa
la sembianza di lei che me a me fura;
s'io vidi il volto orribil di Medusa
far lei contro ad Amor troppo esser dura;
se poi mie mente dal tremor confusa
sotto il tuo schermo diventò secura;
s'Amor con teco a grande opra mi chiama,
mostrami il porto, o dea, d'eterna fama.

XLIII

E tu che drento alla 'nfocata nube
degnasti tua sembianza dimostrarmi,
e ch'ogni altro pensier dal cor mi rube,
fuor che d'amor dal qual non posso atarmi;
e m'infiammasti come a suon di tube
animoso caval s'infiamma all'armi,
fammi in tra gli altri, o Gloria, sí solenne,
ch'io batta insino al cel teco le penne.

XLIV

E s'io son, dolce Amor, s'io son pur degno
essere il tuo campion contro a costei,
contro a costei da cui con forza e 'ngegno,
se ver mi dice il sonno, avinto sei,
fa sí del tuo furor mio pensier pregno,
che spirto di pietà nel cor li crei:
mie virtú per se stessa ha l'ale corte,
perché troppo è 'l valor di costei forte.

41

"O sacrosanct goddess, daughter of Jove, for
whom the temple of Janus opens and closes,
whose powerful right hand holds complete do-
minion over war and peace; holy virgin who
show wondrous proof of your great divinity in
heaven and on earth, you who inflame valorous
hearts to virtue, now help me, Tritonia, give virtue to me.

42

"If I saw enclosed in your armour the features
of her who robs me of myself; if I saw the hor-
rible face of Medusa make her so indomitable
against Love; if later my thoughts, confused by
trembling, became steady behind your shield; if
Love and you are calling me to great deeds,
show me the way, o goddess, to eternal fame.

43

"And you who, inside a fiery cloud, deigned to
show your face to me, who steal every thought
from my heart except for a love which I cannot
help; and you have inflamed me as, at the sound
of trumpets, a spirited horse is inflamed to arms:
make me, o Glory, so excellent among the others that I may beat my wings with you to heaven.

44

"And if I am, sweet Love, if I am indeed worthy
to be your champion against her, against her by
whose force and mind (if my dream has told the
truth) you have been bound, make my thought
so full of your frenzy that a spirit of pity may
be produced in her heart: for my virtue by itself
has wings too short, her prowess is too great.

41/ *the temple of Janus*: In
ancient Rome, the temple of
Janus was opened in times of
war and closed in times of
peace. *Tritonia*: Minerva.

XLV
Troppo forte è, signor, lo suo valore
che, come vedi, el tuo poter non cura;
e tu pur suoli al cor gentile, Amore,
riparar come augello alla verdura.
Ma se mi presti el tuo santo furore,
leverai me sovra la tua natura;
e farai come suol marmorea rota,
che lei non taglia e pure il ferro arruota.

XLVI
Con voi men vegno, Amor Minerva e Gloria,
ché 'l vostro foco tutto el cor m'avampa;
da voi spero acquistar l'alta vittoria,
ché tutto acceso son di vostra lampa;
datemi aita sí ch'ogni memoria
segnar si possa di mia eterna stampa,
e facci umil colei ch'or ne disdegna:
ch'io porterò di voi nel campo insegna.»

45

"Her prowess is too great, my lord, for, as you
see, she pays no heed to yours; and yet you are
accustomed, Love, to take shelter in the noble
heart as a bird among the leaves. But if you lend
me your holy frenzy, you will raise me above
your nature; you will be like a marble wheel,
that cannot cut by itself and yet sharpens a
sword.

46

"I accompany you, Love, Minerva, and Glory,
for your fire inflames all my heart; from you I
hope to gain the lofty victory, for I am all aflame
with your light; give me such aid that every
memory may be sealed with my eternal stamp,
and make her humble who now disdains us: for
yours is the standard I shall carry into the field."

[The poem is unfinished.]

APPENDIX

1

Claudian, *Epithalamium*, 49–91

Mons latus Ionium Cypri praeruptus obumbrat,
invius humano gressu, Phariumque cubile
Proteos et septem despectat cornua Nili.
hunc neque candentes audent vestire pruinae,
hunc venti pulsare timent, hunc laedere nimbi.
luxuriae Venerique vacat. pars acrior anni
exulat; aeterni patet indulgentia veris.
in campum se fundit apex; hunc aurea saepes
circuit et fulvo defendit prata metallo.
Mulciber, ut perhibent, his oscula coniugis emit
moenibus et tales uxorius obtulit arces.
intus rura micant, manibus quae subdita nullis
perpetuum florent, Zephyro contenta colono,
umbrosumque nemus, quo non admittitur ales,
ni probet ante suos diva sub iudice cantus:
quae placuit, fruitur ramis; quae victa, recedit.
vivunt in Venerem frondes omnisque vicissim
felix arbor amat; nutant ad mutua palmae
foedera, populeo suspirat populus ictu
et platani platanis alnoque adsibilat alnus.
   Labuntur gemini fontes, his dulcis, amarus
alter, et infusis corrumpunt mella venenis,
unde Cupidineas armari fama sagittas.
mille pharetrati ludunt in margine fratres,
ore pares, aevo similes, gens mollis Amorum.
hos Nymphae pariunt, illum Venus aurea solum
edidit. ille deos caelumque et sidera cornu
temperat et summos dignatur figere reges;
hi plebem feriunt. nec cetera numina desunt:
hic habitat nullo constricta Licentia nodo
et flecti faciles Irae vinoque madentes
Excubiae Lacrimaeque rudes et gratus amantum
Pallor et in primis titubans Audacia furtis
iucundique Metus et non secura Voluptas;
et lasciva volant levibus Periuria ventis.

1.
Claudian *Epithalamium*, 49–91
(*Stanze* I, 70–96)

A rugged mountain overshadows the Ionian
coast of Cyprus; inaccessible to human foot, it
faces the Pharian den of Proteus and the seven
mouths of the Nile. Gleaming frost dares not
clothe this place; here the winds fear to blow
and the clouds to darken. It is reserved for
pleasure and for Venus. The harsher part of the
year is banished; the blessings of an eternal
spring lie over all. The peak slopes down into a
plain that a golden fence surrounds, protecting
the meadows with yellow metal. Vulcan, so it
is said, purchased the kisses of his wife by offer-
ing her these walls and towers. The fields within
glow; unworked by any hand, they flower eter-
nally, content with Zephyr as their gardener. No
bird is admitted to the shady grove unless it first
tests its song for the judgment of the goddess;
those which please her may flutter in the
branches; the unsuccessful depart. The very
leaves are in love and each happy tree loves in
turn. The palms sway in mutual accord, the poplar breathes its own kind of poplar sigh, plane
tree whispers to plane tree, alder to alder.

    Twin fountains flow, one sweet, the other bit-
ter; they mingle, honey tainted with venom, into
which it is said that Cupid dips his arrows. A
thousand of his quivered brothers play upon the
banks, similar to him in face and age, the tender
band of Loves. These the nymphs bore: Cupid is
the only son of golden Venus. With his bow, he
rules the gods, stars, and heavens, and he deigns
to pierce the greatest among earthly kings; the
Loves wound the common people. Nor are other
deities absent. Here License dwells, restrained by
no fetters, Anger easily enraged and Vigils

quos inter petulans alta cervice Iuventas
excludit Senium luco.
            Procul atria divae
permutant radios silvaque obstante virescunt.
Lemnius haec etiam gemmis extruxit et auro
admiscens artem pretio trabibusque smaragdi
supposuit caesas hyacinthi rupe columnas.
beryllo paries et iaspide lubrica surgunt
limina despectusque solo calcatur achates.

2
Ovid, *Ars Amatoria* I, 527–56

Gnosis in ignotis amens errabat harenis,
    Qua brevis aequoreis Dia feritur aquis.
Utque erat e somno tunica velata recincta,
    Nuda pedem, croceas inreligata comas,
Thesea crudelem surdas clamabat ad undas
    Indigno teneras imbre rigante genas.
Clamabat, flebatique simul, sed utrumque decebat;
    Non facta est lacrimis turpior illa suis.
Iamque iterum tundens mollissima pectora palmis
    "Perfidus ille abiit; quid mihi fiet?" ait.
"Quid mihi fiet?" ait sonuerunt cymbala toto
    Littore, ed adtonita tympana pulsa manu.
Excidit illa metu, rupitque novissima verba;
    Nullus in exanimi corpore sanguis erat.

Ecce Mimallonides sparsis in terga capillis:
    Ecce leves satyri, praevia turba dei:
Ebrius, ecce, senex pando Silenus asello
    Vix sedet, et pressas continet ante iubas.

drenched with wine, naive Tears and Pallor welcome to lovers, Boldness hesitant at its first
intrigue, happy Fears and uncertain Pleasure;
wanton Oaths fly about in the lightest of breezes;
among them all petulant Youth with haughty
bearing excludes Age from the grove.

From afar the house of the goddess shines, re-
flecting the green of the surrounding grove. Vulcan also built this of precious stones, joining
their golden worth to art. Pillars hewn from rock
of hyacinth support emerald beams. The walls
are constructed of beryl and the smooth threshold of jaspar; one looks down and walks on an
agate floor.

2.
Ovid *Ars Amatoria* I, 527–56
(*Stanze* I, 110–12)

Distracted, the Cnossian maid wandered on the
unknown shores, where tiny Naxos is struck by
the waves of the sea. As she awakened, covered
by her loose tunic, barefoot, her golden hair un-
bound, she cried for Theseus to the deaf waves,
moistening her tender cheeks with undeserved
tears. She called out and wept at the same time,
and both became her; she was not made less
beautiful by her tears. And now again beating
her soft little breast with the palms of her hands,
she cries, "That traitor is gone! What will become of me." "What will become of me?" she
cries: frenzied drums and cymbals, struck by
hand, resounded through the whole shore.
Breaking off her last words, she fainted for fear;
no blood was left in her breathless body. Behold
the Bacchae, their hair strewn down their backs,
behold the nimble satyrs, the forerunning throng
of the god; behold the old drunkard Silenus who

Dum sequitur Bacchas, Bacchae fugiuntque petuntqu
    Quadrupedem ferula dum malus urget eques,
In caput aurito cecidit delapsus asello:
    Clamarunt satyri "surge age, surge, pater."
Iam deus in curru, quem summum texerat uvis,
    Tigribus adiunctis aurea lora dabat:
Et color et Theseus et vox abiere puellae:
    Terque fugam petiit, terque retenta metu est.
Horruit, ut steriles agitat quas ventus aristas,
    Ut levis in madida canna palude tremit.
Cui deus "en, adsum tibi cura fidelior" inquit:
    "Pone metum: Bacchi, Gnosias, uxor eris.

3a.
Lucretius, *De Rerum Natura* I, 1–9, 29–40

Aeneadum genetrix, hominum divomque voluptas,
alma Venus, caeli subter labentia signa
quae mare navigerum, quae terras frugiferentis
concelebras, per te quoniam genus omne animantum
concipitus visitque exortum lumina solis:
te, dea, te fugiunt venti, te nubila caeli
adventumque tuum, tibi suavis daedala tellus
submittit flores, tibi rident aequora ponti
placatumque nitet diffuso lumine caelum.

effice ut interea fera moenera militiai
per maria ac terras omnis sopita quiescant.
nam tu sola potes tranquilla pace iuvare
mortalis, quoniam belli fera moenera Mavors

sits with difficulty on his sway-backed donkey,
and holds fast to its mane. He chases the Bacchae who flee and counterattack; and while the
clumsy horseman urges on his steed with a stick,
he slips and falls headlong from the long-eared
donkey. The satyrs cry, "Get up! Come on father, get up!" Now the god in his chariot, the
top of which was covered with grape leaves,
slackens the golden reins about his yoked tigers:
Theseus, her voice, her color, all leave the girl:
three times she seeks flight and three times is
held back by fear. She trembles as dry stalks
shaken by the wind, as light cane trembles in a
wet marsh. To whom the god said, "Lo, my love
is a more faithful one; put away fear, maid of
Cnossos, you will be the wife of Bacchus."
(See also another Ovidian treatment of Ariadne
in *Heroides* X, and an earlier version of the same
myth in Catullus LXIV, 50–264)

3a.
Lucretius, *De Rerum Natura* I, 1–9, 29–40
(*Stanze* I, 122)

Mother of Aeneas, delight of men and gods, benign Venus! under the wandering signs of heaven,
you give life to the ship-bearing sea and the
fruitful earth; through your power, every living
creature is conceived and opens its newborn eyes
to the sunlight. The winds flee from you, Goddess, the clouds of heaven fly from your coming;
the resourceful earth places flowers beneath
your feet. The surface of the sea smiles for you,
and the calmed heavens shine with a radiant
light.
   Meanwhile let the fierce activity of war on sea
and on land everywhere be laid to rest. For you
alone can bring quiet to mortal men; powerful

armipotens regit, in gremium qui saepe tuum se
reicit aeterno devictus vulnere amoris,
atque ita suspiciens tereti cervice reposta
pascit amore avidos inhians in te, dea, visus
eque tuo pendet resupini spiritus ore.
hunc tu, diva, tuo recubantem corpore sancto
circumfusa super, suavis ex ore loquellas
funde petens placidam Romanis, incluta, pacem.

3b.
Marsilio Ficino, *Commentary on the Symposium:
De Amore*, from Oration v, Chapter 8

. . . Mars fortitudine praestat, quia fortiores
homines efficit. Venus hunc domat. Quando
enim Mars in angulis caeli, vel secunda nativitatis
domo, vel octava constitutus nascenti mala por-
tendit, Venus saepe coniunctione sua, vel oppo-
sitione, vel receptione aut aspectu sextile, aut
trino, Martis, ut ita dicamus, compescit maligni-
tatem. Rursus quando Mars in ortu hominis
dominatur, magnitudinem animi iracundiamque
largitur. Si proxime Venus accesserit, virtutem
illam magni animi a Marte datam non impedit,
sed vitium iracundiae reprimit. Ubi clementio-
rem facere Martem et domare videtur. *Mars
autem Venerem numquam domat.*

Mars, who rules the savagery of war, often throws himself into your lap, vanquished by the eternal wound of love; and thus, gazing upward, his handsome neck curved back, fixing his hungry eyes upon you, he feeds them on love; prostrate, his breath hangs upon your lips. Wind your sacred body about him, glorious goddess, as he lies recumbent, and let your lips speak sweetly, imploring a tranquil peace for the Romans.

3b.
Marsilio Ficino, *Commentary on the Symposium: De Amore*, from Oration V, chapter 8

. . . Mars stands foremost in strength for he makes men stronger. Yet Venus masters him. When Mars, stationed in the angle of heaven, either in the second or the eighth house, portends misfortune to the newborn child, Venus, in conjunction with him, in opposition to him, or in reception either in the sextile or trine aspect, so to speak, often restrains his malignance. Again, when Mars is dominant at a man's birth, he imparts to him greatness of soul and irascibility; if Venus comes next in influence, she does not hinder that virtue of a great soul given by Mars, but she does suppress the vice of irascibility. Wherefore she seems to tame and placate Mars. *But Mars never masters Venus.*

Bibliography

Ida Maier's *Ange Politien* (Geneva, 1966) is a modern biography of Poliziano; however, it covers only the period from 1469 to 1480 in depth. For a lively biographical sketch of the poet in English, see Alan Moorehead's essay, "The Angel in May," *The New Yorker,* February 1951, 34–65. For discussions of Poliziano's scholarly career, see Eugenio Garin, "The Cultural Background of Politian," in Garin, *Portraits from the Quattrocento* (New York, 1972), 161–89, A. Grafton, "On the Scholarship of Politian and Its Context," *Journal of the Warburg and Courtauld Institutes* 40 (1977): 150–88, and the chapter on Poliziano in Grafton, *Joseph Scaliger: A Study in the History of Classical Scholarship 1: Textual Criticism and Exegesis* (Oxford, 1983), 9–44; Jill Kraye, "Cicero, Stoicism, and Textual Criticism: Poliziano on Katorthoma," *Rinascimento* 23 (1983): 79–110; Vittore Branca, *Poliziano e l'umanesimo della parola* (Turin, 1983); and the essays collected in *Il Poliziano e il suo tempo* (Florence, 1957). In 1972 Branca and Manlio Pastore Stocchi published the hitherto unknown second part of Poliziano's *Miscellanea,* the *Miscellaneorum Centuria Secunda* (Florence, 1972), 4 vols. Recent years have seen a spate of critical editions of Poliziano's manuscript commentaries in Latin on ancient texts; these allow a reconstruction of his philological methods. See the *Commento inedito all'epistola ovidiana di Saffo a Faone,* ed. Elisabetta Lazzeri (Florence, 1971): *La commedia antica e l'Andria di Terenzio: Appunti inediti,* ed. Rosetta Lattanza Roselli (Florence, 1973); *Commento inedito alle Selve di Stazio,* ed. Lucia Cesarini Martinelli (Florence, 1978); *Commento inedito alle Satire di Persio,* ed. Lucia Cesarini Martinelli and Roberto Ricciardi (Città di Castello, 1985); *Commento inedito ai Fasti di Ovidio,* ed. Francesco Lo Monaco (Florence, 1991). For a discussion of Poliziano's translation of Homer, see Alice Levine Rubinstein, "Imitation and Style in Angelo Poliziano's *Iliad* Translation," *Renaissance Quarterly* 36 (1983): 48–70.

The critical edition of the *Stanze* of Vincenzo Pernicone (Turin, 1954) has been reprinted by Bruno Maier, *Stanze per la Giostra, Orfeo, Rime* (Novara, 1968). Natalino Sapegno has revised the Pernicone text in his edition of the *Rime* (1967). The serious student of the *Stanze* will find indispensable both Giosue Carducci's commentary to his edition of Poliziano's works, *Le Stanze, l'Orfeo, e le Rime di Messer Angelo Ambrogini Poliziano* (Florence, 1863), and the supplementary notes provided by Sapegno in his *Commento alle Rime del Poliziano* (Rome, 1952–53). These notes are reprinted in Sapegno's edition of the *Rime*.

Eugenio Donato has written about the *Stanze*'s dialectical relationship to history in "Death and History in Poliziano's *Stanze*," *MLN* 80 (1965): 27–40. In *The Earthly Paradise and the Renaissance Epic* (Princeton, 1966), 129–34, A. Bartlett Giamatti relates the garden of Venus to its literary tradition, dwelling on the theme of erotic subjugation. Giamatti's reading is criticized by Ronnie H. Terpening in "Poliziano's Treatment of a Classical Topos: Ekphrasis, Portal to the *Stanze*," *Italian Quarterly* 67 (1974). Thomas M. Greene offers an important critical treatment of the *Stanze* in the chapter devoted to Poliziano in his *The Light in Troy: Imitation and Discovery in Renaissance Poetry* (New Haven, 1982), 147–70. Renzo Lo Cascio presents a detailed discussion of Poliziano's handling of his source materials in *Lettura del Poliziano: Le "Stanze per la giostra"* (Palermo, 1954). Neoplatonic interpretations of the poem are offered in two articles by Arnolfo Ferruolo: "A Trend in Renaissance Thought and Art: Poliziano's *Stanze per la Giostra*," *The Romanic Review* 44 (1953): 246–56, and "Botticelli's Mythologies, Ficino's *De Amore*, Poliziano's *Stanze per la Giostra*: Their Circle of Love," *Art Bulletin* 37 (1955): 16–25, and by Sandra L. Bermann, "Neoplatonism in Politian's *Stanze per la giostra*," *Forum Italicum* 15 (1981): 11–21.

For Poliziano's literary relationship with Lorenzo de' Medici, the reader can now consult an anthology of the latter's writings that has been translated into English: *Lorenzo de' Medici: Selected Poems and Prose*, ed. Jon Thiem (University Park, Pa., 1991).

On the relationship of Poliziano and Botticelli, see the fundamental studies by Charles Dempsey, "*Mercurius ver:* The Sources of Botticelli's *Primavera,*" *Journal of the Warburg and Courtauld Institutes* 31 (1968): 251–73, and by Pierre Francastel, "La fête mythologique au Quattrocento: Expression littéraire et visualisation plastique," in Francastel, *La réalité figurative: Eléments structurels de sociologie de l'art* (Paris, 1965), 241–71. Dempsey has expanded and revised his arguments in *The Portrayal of Love: Botticelli's "Primavera" and Humanist Culture at the Time of Lorenzo the Magnificent* (Princeton, 1992). See also the pioneering work of Abby Warburg, *Sandro Botticellis "Geburt der Venus" und "Frühling"* (Leipzig, 1893), and for a further discussion, Edgar Wind, *Pagan Mysteries in the Renaissance* (New York, 1968), 113–40. A less persuasive argument is found in E. H. Gombrich, "Botticelli's Mythologies: A Study in the Neoplatonic Symbolism of His Circles," in Gombrich, *Symbolic Images* (London, 1972), 31–81.